D1557589

BETWEEN RIGHT AND RIGHT

By A. B. Yehoshua

THREE DAYS AND A CHILD
EARLY IN THE SUMMER OF 1970
THE LOVER
BETWEEN RIGHT AND RIGHT

BETWEEN RIGHT AND RIGHT

A. B. YEHOSHUA

*Translated
from the Hebrew
by Arnold Schwartz*

1981
Doubleday & Company, Inc.
Garden City, New York

ISBN: 0-385-17035-1
Library of Congress Catalog Card Number: 80-721
Originally published in Israel as *Bizcut Hanormaliut,*
Copyright © 1980 by Schocken Publishing House, Ltd.,
Tel Aviv
Translation copyright © 1981 by A. B. Yehoshua

CONTENTS

PREFACE   vii

THE HOLOCAUST AS JUNCTION   1

THE *GOLAH:* THE NEUROTIC SOLUTION   21

BETWEEN RIGHT AND RIGHT:
   ONE RIGHT AND ANOTHER'S   75

JEW, ISRAELI, ZIONIST: HONING
   THE CONCEPTS   107

THE CONSTANT SHADOW OF WAR   149

PREFACE

If fifteen years ago someone had told me that one day I would publish a collection of essays on Zionism, I would have dismissed him with an indulgent smile. At that time I considered Zionism a closed book. It had proven itself, made itself clear politically and historically, and had been acknowledged by most of humankind. Since the Six-Day War, however, we have come to realize that questions we thought decided were not decided—not for ourselves and not for the outside world; that matters which for us were simple and straightforward are not all that simple and straightforward. The political debate on the future of the territories in western Eretz Israel occupied in the war became no more than a chink through which the depths of controversy and interpretation, intention and fantasy, their roots reaching down to the very beginning of Jewish history, were exposed once again. I, along with friends who shared my way of thinking, felt compelled to take part in the debates and deliberations, which were becoming increasingly acrimonious. I had to redefine a number of fundamental concepts in my life as an individual and a Jew, to clarify the true meanings of positions, and to mark out a direction for the future. All this was done with a sense of urgency. If I and others who share my views did not clarify those views, others would do it for us, and sooner or later we would be pressed into a corner, unable to breathe.

I am not a historian or a Jewish philosopher, nor am I a scholar of either Zionism or the Holocaust, and I have no pretensions about making scientific or scholarly statements on these matters. The welcome recent developments in Jewish studies, especially in some schools where those studies are based on new research into Zionism and the Holocaust, cannot exempt the Israeli, as an individual, from considering these questions for himself. This he must do to form a coherent world view. The Diaspora, the Holocaust, the moral issues raised by the Arab-Israeli conflict—these are not only issues for scholars and experts. They are part of our spiritual being, part of the personal identity of each of us. Although a great store of knowledge has been amassed in recent years in a large number of studies, there are still general questions which, for reasons of caution, researchers do not dare ask themselves, linkages and connections they hesitate to make.

I am not a believer in debate for its own sake. I hold, rather, that there most definitely are clear and unambiguous answers, that there are precise definitions, that it is possible to make clear moral judgments. The historical facts, the sense of natural justice, and common sense are excellent tools and are available to all. In this book I have tried to present clear answers, unhesitatingly, knowing full well that some of them will give rise to considerable objection.

These essays began in lectures, symposia, public debates, and interviews with the media. The polemical tone of the lecture and debate still sounds between the lines. I want to express my sincerest gratitude to all those unnamed persons—university colleagues, youths, kibbutz members, soldiers, disputants at symposia, and others—who by debating, objecting, and questioning and by their illuminating comments helped me better clarify my own thoughts. I also owe a debt of gratitude to my friend Ilan Eldar of Haifa University who was kind enough to go over the manuscript and make his very useful comments.

Haifa, February 1980

BETWEEN
RIGHT
AND
RIGHT

THE HOLOCAUST AS JUNCTION

Before the Yom Kippur War, in a symposium conducted by the Israel Defense Forces, scholars seriously discussed various questions raised by the Holocaust. To conclude the proceedings, the moderator addressed the following question to the participants: "Gentlemen, today we stand at a distance of thirty years from this vast mountain, the Holocaust, and the further in time we get from it, the higher it appears. How do you envisage the Holocaust's influence on the Jewish people in the future?"

Professor Yehuda Bauer replied: "Judging by the experience of the last twenty-five years, the Holocaust's influence has not waned. And in light of what has been said here, neither has the danger of a recurrence of the Holocaust passed. Study and research of the Holocaust period will continue to be an intellectual and emotional challenge in the future as well. Our future generations, the heirs of the

Holocaust generation, will undoubtedly raise many incisive
questions. How did that generation endure the Holocaust?
How did it act, passively and actively? Did it manage to
preserve a human semblance, and if so, how? These questions, I am sure, will occupy future generations. Furthermore, it seems to me that the shock and horror aroused by
the mere knowledge that human beings can sink to such a
level as to be able to treat others with such incredible cruelty will spark thoughts leading in new directions and will
intensify the drive to find an answer to the question: How
could such a thing have happened?"

The late Professor Ben-Sasson summed up his remarks:
"Up until now the Jewish people, and likewise Christianity
and Islam, has always known how to transform the memory of disasters into assets, into creativity. This has not yet
been done for the Holocaust. And however harsh and cruel
it may sound, this horrible experience called the Holocaust
also must be made a part of our culture. The truth is that
until now we have grappled only very slightly with the Holocaust. Thirty years later, there is a great deal we have yet
to examine; what has been revealed up until now is only
the tip of the iceberg. You ask how the Holocaust will
influence the Jewish people in the future. This depends first
of all on how the Jewish people will develop and on how
this component will be fitted into the mosaic of its development and culture. Here another question arises: Will the
Jewish people harness the tremendous strength needed to
build this experience into its culture? In any event, the
three factors I have mentioned—converting the influence of
the Holocaust from negative to creative; fitting the Holocaust into the fabric of the people's culture; and, as a
condition for both of these, the grappling for and with
knowledge—these will determine how the Holocaust will influence the character of the Jewish people in the future."

And Professor Saul Friedlander said: "The absence of a
meaningful coming to terms with the traumatic experience
of the Holocaust stems, in my view, from a phenomenon
quite well known in clinical psychology, although it is perhaps difficult to draw parallels here between the individual
and a community. When a child undergoes a severely traumatic experience, it frequently happens that in the child-
hood years that follow, in the years of his development as a
youth, the effects of that trauma are hardly discernible, except perhaps for small marginal effects. The grave consequences often reveal themselves only much later, when he
reaches a level of some maturity. It then becomes apparent
that the primary shock was followed by a quiescent period
of repression. Similarly, it seems to me that we have not yet
grappled with the Holocaust on a number of planes because we are not yet able to. Despite the many studies conducted, in this field we are still in a kind of paralysis. When
we discover and publish new documents in this field, if
they awaken a response at all it is only an initial response;
the true coming to terms has not yet begun. I find support
for this in, among other things, the poverty of the literature
on the Holocaust that has appeared until now, with perhaps several exceptions that only point up the rule. The
time is not yet ripe for the emotional coming to terms. All
this gives me a strong sense that we are still in the period
of repression, that the experience in all its severity will yet
break through to the surface. When that happens we will
truly feel its impress."

These remarks were made about nine years ago. The
time that has elapsed since then has confirmed that the
speakers were right. The Yom Kippur War removed another barrier of repression and created another historical
context for identification with the Holocaust. But even put-
ting aside the impact of the Yom Kippur War, the feeling

is that interest in the Holocaust, and the events of the Holocaust, has greatly increased and that the primary repression clamped down immediately after World War II is beginning to give way. Over the last years we have seen the Holocaust memorial days become more genuine. Institutes for the study of the Holocaust have been set up in the universities, and the Holocaust has become an academic discipline in its own right. New films, such as *The Eighty-first Blow,* have enabled a broad public to establish fresh contact with this painful subject. Hebrew literature, which in the years following World War II totally ignored the subject, has begun to take it up, from a variety of angles and in new aesthetic forms. And as if some hidden obstacle had been cleared away for them, writers who themselves went through the Holocaust, but who earlier did not write a word about it, are now beginning to record their experiences of that period. This is happening not only among Israelis or Jews. There is tremendous interest in the Holocaust throughout the world. Historical works and biographies of major figures from the period are appearing with increasing frequency in the West. The American TV series "Holocaust," although mediocre, awakened a tide of the most profound feeling among hundreds of millions of viewers around the world. The history of World War II and of the Holocaust has been made part of the compulsory school curriculum in many countries. The President of the United States formed a special committee to perpetuate the memory of the Holocaust in the United States and appointed a special adviser for this. In American, German, and French literature we are witness to a tide of books by young authors who, although they themselves were born after the war, have made it their central experience. In Eastern Europe and Soviet Russia, World War II is still a foremost focus of national identification. Let us not forget that the Second World War was the last war experienced by many peoples and its impact has yet to be supplanted by some other experience.

This preoccupation with the Holocaust stems, I think, from something uniquely associated with it. As an event it contains much that is deeply perplexing and incomprehensible. It is this essential incomprehensibility—inevitable, given the event's demonic nature—which, I think, is at the root of the obsessional preoccupation with the Holocaust. There have been many and varied attempts to attack this subject from a number of directions, but still a sense of satisfaction, that calm which comes with closure, cannot be achieved. Intellectual and emotional disquiet will be with us for a long time yet. Although the pile of documents and researches continues to mount, the bulk of the iceberg beneath the surface gets no smaller.

We can expect continued study of the Holocaust to raise new, difficult, and disturbing questions, some of which we have not yet encountered. But no taboo of the sort "We have no right to judge the dead" can be allowed to be imposed. We can anticipate that this subject will give rise to bizarre speculations and fantastic theories proffering new answers. Attempts at explanation by referring to "collaboration" and the "banality of evil" are just the first inklings of this. Art and literature, too, have gone off into the territory of perverse experience in order to create a new identificatory shock. As the number of surviving eyewitnesses to the period diminishes, the more freely will human imagination range in its attempts to achieve understanding. All this will have to be met in a spirit of patience and openness. The horror of the events and the sufferings of the victims will not rob the new attempts—including new emotional and moral judgments—of legitimacy. The freedom of man's spirit suffers no restriction. Hence we must be aware that further study is liable to inflict new pain and will sometimes require that generally accepted views, which, it seemed, were firmly and solidly established, be abandoned.

IDEOLOGICAL JUNCTION

No one is exempt from having to reexamine his view of the world following the Holocaust. It was not just another historical event that we sort into ready-made categories of one or another world view. The world after the Holocaust is not the same as the world before the Holocaust. Mankind's horizon has been pushed back and some of the fundamental concepts we live with have now to be reinspected. We, the Jews, in particular have to do this. The Holocaust has confronted us with some of the most difficult questions that can be raised. These require new answers, or at least call for adjustments in the old answers. But we should realize that the experience of the Holocaust can serve to reinforce different, and at times opposing, world views. It is for this reason that we must view the Holocaust as a vast historical junction from which roads lead off in various directions. Following any one of these roads is justifiable on the basis of this or that aspect, of this or that lesson drawn from the profound and complex darkness of that awesome event.

The Holocaust can be apprehended in metaphysical terms as demonstrating the inability of the rational mind to grasp and understand the world. The Holocaust thus reinforces the religious conception: as in God's answer to Job, the world of the Holocaust can be approached only by way of religious concepts. Despite the mortal blow received by the Jewish people in the Holocaust, the nation still exists, and that is additional proof of the special Divine Providence that watches over and accompanies it. On the basis of the experience of the Holocaust, the religious Jew can heighten his faith and sense clearly the grace of God. Just a small step stood between the people and total destruction, and yet it has risen and has shaken off the ashes. A sense of God's omnipotence can emerge in the wake of the Holocaust.

But another path, no less clear, also leads out from that same crossroads. The Holocaust was the final and conclusive proof that there is not and never was a God in heaven. How can any theological belief that speaks of Divine Providence, of reward and punishment, of divine grace, be maintained after the slaughter of a million children in the concentration camps? What meaning can religious sin have, given the Nazis' total nondiscrimination between the righteous and the evil, between those who observed the commandments and those who denied God's existence? And what remains of the uniqueness of the Jewish people, for did not the Gypsies suffer a similar fate? If someone doubted the existence of God prior to the Holocaust, the Holocaust provided him with final confirmation of his doubts.

World War II provided conclusive proof of the nature and meaning of international relations. In the final analysis the world is a big jungle, values have no meaning, international law has no meaning. Might is right. World War II demonstrated the true value of international guarantees and the worth of signed agreements. The inescapable conclusion to be drawn from the experience of the war is that every nation must depend only on itself, must be strong and always on the alert against attack and treachery. Don't make concessions in return for fine-sounding assurances,

don't pay heed to values of international justice. In this
world *homo homini lupus* (man is a wolf to man), and if
you want to survive you, too, must be a strong and alert
wolf.

However, the very opposite view can also be justified on
the basis of the experience of World War II. Behold what
selfish and brutal nationalism leads us to. Constant striving
to reform the world offers the only chance for survival. We
Jews must be active partners in the reform of the world. It
is necessary to strengthen the international organizations,
to foster the brotherhood of peoples, to merge races and
peoples. In the final analysis the free world triumphed over
the Nazi beast not only in strength but also in spirit. That
victory is a source of hope for a new order, and only by
preserving that order and shoring up the values of justice is
there any chance of staving off a recurrence of Nazism.

The Holocaust also provided indisputable proof to all
those who hold to notions of a unique Jewish destiny. How
much our destiny and place in the world differ from those
of other peoples became most horribly apparent in World
War II. The yellow badge affixed to the Jew's garment was
but a physical representation of what had always been
known: that we are different. To seek to escape this singular destiny is futile—this the Holocaust proved. The
different historical path of the Jewish people was only
made emphatically more apparent by the horrible experience of the Holocaust.

But on the basis of that same experience others will say
that the Holocaust proved once and for all the urgency of
normalization of the Jewish people, the need to be a nation
in the family of nations with equal rights and obligations.
Here is the unequivocal Zionist conception demanding
normalization of our existence, and there stand those who
prove beyond a shadow of doubt that our unique historical

destiny requires that we be dispersed among the nations: "How charitable was God in scattering us among the nations," for had we not been dispersed we would have been totally annihilated in World War II.

The Holocaust can provide convincing proof of the utter impossibility of escaping from Jewish identity. Jews who tried to assimilate or deny their identity were forcibly returned to the fold of their people. Better, then, that we all freely identify as Jews; united among ourselves we will be able to confront any similar visitation in the future more honorably and with greater courage.

Nor can we begrudge those who from the same facts arrive at the opposite conclusion, those who argue that if such is the special destiny of the Jewish people, better to flee it while there is still time. Their conclusion from the experience of the Holocaust is rapid flight from this people; in that way at least their offspring will escape a similar fate in the future, just as the offspring of Jews who assimilated in earlier generations escaped the Holocaust.

Here I have indicated only some of the possible opposing interpretations, each based on the same complex historical experience that unfolded before us in World War II. The same facts lead in opposite directions: despair of the world or faith in it and a desire to reform it. A firmer belief in God's mysterious power or total loss of faith. Destiny or freedom. Normalization of Jewish existence or further conclusive proof of the abnormality of that existence. Every interpretation has its reasons, every interpretation its proof. The experience of the Holocaust as a vast junction allows for a multitude of historical conclusions. Small wonder, then, that in Israel, for example, both the extreme Right and the Left have adopted the Holocaust as a powerful focus for identification.

At this awesome junction each person must make his

own ideological decision and set out on the road he has chosen. He must bear in mind, however, that his path is just one of many, and despite his ideological opposition to the other routes, he must acknowledge the legitimacy of contradictory interpretations of the experience of the Holocaust. The ideological struggle between interpretations, between the historical lessons drawn from the Holocaust, must be conducted, if not with a measure of hesitation, then at least with tolerance and respect. Before this tremendously powerful event the stature of each of us is bent low.

But as long as we construct a world view based on the Holocaust, and try to incorporate it into an all-embracing structure, to make it at least the cornerstone of a world view—for that is the test of a genuine coming to terms with the Holocaust (as Professor Ben-Sasson correctly said, "This horrible experience called the Holocaust also must be made a part of our culture")—we must be careful not to establish simple and irresponsible linkages among concepts, facts, and symbols of the Holocaust and those of other fields. Not every minor dictator is a Hitler, and not every anti-Semite is a Nazi. The attempt to intensify opposition by having recourse to analogies from the World War II era can only diminish the force of the facts of the Holocaust events themselves. Let us not forget, the Nazi horror was immeasurably greater than the horrors committed afterward. The combination Hiroshima-Auschwitz, for example, is not proper. The dropping of an atom bomb cannot be included in the same category as the horror of Auschwitz. The Hiroshima incident was clearly a wartime operation, however extreme, against a cruel aggressor, an ally of the Hitlerian fiend, whereas in Auschwitz brutal genocide was carried out on the basis of racist theory. We must be very cautious when incorporating images from the world of the Holocaust into our lives. The context in which the Holocaust took place, its awesome scope and power, must not be forgotten. Comparing Soviet with Nazi persecutions of the Jews only serves to diminish the enormity of the Nazi madness. Talk of the PLO as a Nazi organization only obscures the essential difference between the Nazi madness, the anti-Semitic consistency of murdering every Jew simply because he is a Jew, and the (admittedly cruel) nationalist struggle to oust us from a certain territory.

We, the sons of the victims, we who must not forget, we of all people must be faithful to factual accuracy, to the proper proportions of historical events.

THE BURDEN OF THE HOLOCAUST

The ideological conception I shall try to present is but one such conception, but in my view it is the only one by which a Jew can continue to live after the Holocaust.

First of all, I view the Holocaust as part of history. I say part of history because attempts have been made to describe it as being somehow outside the course of history, an exception to the rules of history that operated until then, a disruption of normal comprehensible processes. I do not see it that way. The Holocaust, it is true, was the nadir, but it is part of a chain of events following a set pattern ever since we went into exile. It marks the climax of a conflict that has always been going on, without ceasing, between the Jewish people and the world. That is why, despite its awesome scope and intensity, the Holocaust was not a one-time occurrence. Based on historical facts that still obtain, it can recur.

THE HOLOCAUST IS THE FINAL DECISIVE
PROOF OF THE FAILURE OF DIASPORA EXIST-
ENCE.

If anyone had illusions about our ability to find our
place in the world as a people scattered among the nations,
the Holocaust provided the final proof of where this form
of existence is likely to lead us.

To all believers that it is the mission of the Jewish people, by this form of existence, to disseminate some spiritual
message among the world's nations, the Holocaust demonstrated the nations' true response to this calling. And what
could be more symbolic than that it was precisely the Germans, among whom we had such a sublime sense of spiritual vocation accompanied by elaborate theories of spiritual
symbiosis (witness Hermann Cohen and others, and the
place the Jews occupied in German cultural and intellectual life on the eve of the Holocaust), that it was they of
all people who presented us with this resounding reply.

But most horrendous of all is that the situation into
which we were cast by the Holocaust came about with no
"choice" whatsoever on our part. In the Crusades or the
Inquisition, for example, we could say that we brought per-
secution upon ourselves out of steadfastness to our faith
and to sanctify our world view. Faced with the choice of
conversion, we chose to remain Jews, and paid the price of
death. In the Holocaust even this "choice" was denied us
and we cannot say that by our deaths we sanctified the
name of God, for we had no alternative. We were not even
given the freedom to choose death. Death was forced on
us. It was forced on those who believed in God and on
those who did not believe in God; it was forced on those
who identified as Jews and on those who did not want to
identify as Jews. Our death was decreed for the absurd
reason of our being a race, which of course we never were.

The Holocaust made an absurdity of our existence and beliefs.

The Jewish people's terrible sacrifice in the Holocaust was for no purpose. The Hebrew word *shoah*, with its echoes of utter devastation, expresses the nature of this sacrifice immeasurably better than the word *holocaust*, a Christian term for a whole burnt offering, a sin offering by someone for something. Those whom the concentration camp flames consumed did not die for any idea, for any world view; they did not meet their deaths for the continued existence of the Jewish people or for its imminent redemption. There are some who say, or at least try to console themselves by saying, that it was the Holocaust that, as it were, begat the State of Israel. This assertion I reject totally, on both factual and moral grounds. The State of Israel could also have been established had there been no Holocaust. In fact, the State of Israel would today be much, much stronger had a third of its people not been wiped out. And on moral grounds, the Holocaust simply cannot be accepted by virtue of the later establishment of the State of Israel. If we were confronted with the choice: no Holocaust and therefore no State of Israel, I doubt that any of us would dare say: Let there be a Holocaust so that the State of Israel can be established.

The Holocaust proved to us the danger of our abnormal existence among the nations, the danger of the nonlegitimacy of our presence among the nations. It was easy for the Nazis to destroy us and to get other peoples to participate in our destruction, either actively or by acquiescence, because our status in the world was not legitimate. We were outside of history, we were not "like all the nations." Because by our ways of life we were "other," different from all others, it was easy to regard us as subhuman, and as subhuman our blood could be spilled freely. The first to be seized upon in any national shock, in any instance of social unrest, were the Jews.

The Nazi madness was only an extreme manifestation of the collective psychopathology that emerges, or is liable to emerge, in response to the ambiguity of the Jews' existence among the nations. The unclear identity of part of the people, our dual loyalty to the nation among whom we live and to the Jewish people scattered among many countries, our attachment to another homeland—all these are always potential foci of conflict in times of national crisis, and over them we have no control. Tolerance, humanism, religious pluralism are all thin protective layers that quickly crumble when national interest or social crisis presses upon them.

The essential lack of clarity of our situation in the world, the lack of clarity also about our intentions (our own lack of clarity about them), bring out pathological aggression from those historical forces unable to endure ambiguity.

The Holocaust bared the profound hazards of the Jew's situation in the world. The solution is not to change the world, to bring it into line with the special nature of our existence, but to change the nature of Jewish existence, to bring it into line with the world. The solution is normalization of Jewish existence.

All those who try to present the Holocaust as another expression of Jewish destiny are in fact asserting that this pattern of relations is irremediable, that we have no control over our destiny, that we move on a course without exit. This conception sought, for example, to unite in one memorial day both Holocaust Day and the Ninth of Av (a day of fasting in memory of the destruction of the Second Temple and the exile from Spain). That is to obfuscate the essential difference between, on the one hand, the destruction of the Temple and the loss of independence and, on

the other, the Holocaust as the failure of Diaspora existence. These are two totally different events. The destruction of the Second Temple represents the failure of our way
of conducting our independence, the failure of our exces-
sive activism as a nation among nations. The Holocaust
represents the failure of the terrible passivity of our scattered exilic existence among the nations. Between these
two colossal failures we must find a third, more proper way
to exist among the world's peoples.

THE CHALLENGE OF THE HOLOCAUST

But the Holocaust, while laying a heavy burden on us, also
confronts us with challenges. As the sons of the victims, it
is our duty to be the bearers of several clear lessons. These
we must bring to the world.

The first lesson is profound rejection of racism and chauvinism. Having experienced in the flesh the price of racism
and extreme nationalism, we must reject their manifestations not only in the past, not only among ourselves. We
must reject them everywhere and among all peoples. We
must be the standard-bearers of opposition to racism in all
its forms and manifestations. Nazism was not only a German phenomenon. It is a general human phenomenon, and
no people, and I stress *no people,* is immune to it.

After World War II it was asked how such a cultured
and developed people as were the Germans, a people that
had produced geniuses of intellect and artistic creation, de-
generated to a level of such execrable crime. A number of
historians and German "experts" advanced the proposition
that Nazism has always been present, potentially, in the
Germans, that the Nazi view of the world is rooted in the

German spirit and mentality. This theory tried to prove that the nature of the German people is such that it is potentially criminal, that the unique German combination of powerful nationalism, a sense of order, and blind obedience is itself capable of breeding Nazism. In this view the Germans cannot be other than what they are and are always foredoomed to criminality. For that reason they must always be kept under close watch and on a short leash to prevent another outburst of mad violence. What is more, on the basis of this argument, the Germans cannot possibly be held morally responsible for their deeds. What they did is part of their nature from birth.

The years that have elapsed since World War II, it seems, have proved theories of this sort wrong. Present-day Germany (I refer to democratic Western Germany) is a different Germany. It is a country of freedom, democracy, and strict respect for individual rights. As such, it is conclusive proof that Nazism is not inevitable for the Germans but is an outlook and way of life that they *chose*. Hence they are morally responsible for it. Let it not be forgotten that Hitler was elected by great numbers of the German people and they cooperated with him along his entire course. That Germany can in fact be different indicates that Nazism was not imposed on it but was chosen by it. And therefore the Germans are historically and morally responsible for what happened.

But the years that have elapsed have also demonstrated, to our deep sorrow, that the phenomenon of Nazism is possible among other peoples as well. True, the horrors have not yet reached the heights of World War II, but events in Biafra, Bangladesh, and Cambodia are not so distant from the scale of the Nazi butchery.

We, as victims of the Nazi infection, must be the bearers of the antibodies to this horrible disease which is liable to attack any people. And as the bearers of these antibodies we must first of all be careful regarding ourselves.

At the same time we must also be careful not to lose a sense of proportion and not to measure everything by comparison with the Holocaust. Having suffered such a horrendous experience, we are liable to grow indifferent to any lesser suffering. He who has suffered greatly may become inured to the suffering of others. That is completely natural. But as the bearers of the anti-Nazi message we must whet our sensitivity, not dull it. We must bear in mind that our having been victims does not accord us any special moral standing. The victim does not become virtuous for having been a victim. Although the Holocaust inflicted a horrible injustice on us, it did not grant us a certificate of everlasting righteousness. The murderers were amoral; the victims were not made moral. To be moral you must behave ethically. The test of that is daily and constant.

I have already noted that the Holocaust can lead an individual to despair of the world. After the experience of the Holocaust it is natural to be left with no faith in man or his actions. We, the sons of the victims, have a redoubled right to express our profound disappointment with the world. But this, too, we should remember, that despair of the world is a Nazi stance, that Nazism also was born of a feeling that by its nature the world is valueless, that good cannot be expected of man, that the only valid values are might and cunning. Whoever arrives at a nihilistic stance in wake of the experience of the Holocaust paradoxically deeply confirms an implicit Nazi thesis. To be bearers of hope and faith in man is not easy after the Holocaust, but if we wish to be consistent in our anti-Nazism we must take up this challenge as well.

When we study the Holocaust and wonder how it was at all possible, we come to realize how meager was our knowledge of the horrors during the war itself. We sometimes ask ourselves how it is possible that large parts of the people (including the Jewish community in Eretz Israel) had no knowledge of what was going on in occupied Europe. And had we had more knowledge of what was happening, would we have found a way to help more? The problem of blocked channels of communication is not only an objective problem, a situation imposed by the iron hand of a totalitarianism which made sure that the horrors would be concealed from the world's view. It also stemmed from an inner refusal to know what was happening, a refusal to search for every crumb of information that could provide a clearer picture of what was going on. The importance of human communication, the opening of channels of communication, the fostering of the press and other modes of communication are one of the clear lessons of this period. It seems to me that the world after the Holocaust, the Western world, has understood this and is doing what it can to ensure that concealment will no longer be possible. The struggle for unrestricted communication is one of the most important efforts being made to prevent a recurrence of such horrors. We have seen this in our struggle for the fate of Soviet Jewry; we see it in other struggles. Again, as the bearers of the anti-Nazi and antitotalitarian message we must be in the forefront of the fight for the free flow of information and ideas. Whoever tries to silence expression, even for reasons of security and solidarity, in the final analysis sows the seeds of calamity. An open society with a roily flow of information is preferable to denial, concealment, and obfuscation.

And in the final analysis, although the Holocaust is a distinctly Jewish experience, it has eternal meaning for mankind as a whole. Even after many years have passed, man will return to study this period, for the events of this terri-

ble war enlarged the concept of man, expanded the horizon
of human possibilities. It taught us things we did not know
about man's nature. The concept of man, for good or for
evil, after the Holocaust is not the same as the concept of
man prior to the Holocaust. We understand man better
after the Holocaust. True, we always knew that man was
capable of both the most awful evil and the most wondrous
good; still, the Holocaust revealed a new depth of evil to
which man is capable of descending. But it also revealed
man's ability to endure. Walking skeletons in the concentration camps, who biologically were deemed virtually
"dead," still made moral decisions and shared their last
crust of bread with others. Thus, alongside the most awful
despair, hope, too, can be born. We who were there and
came out from there can, and in my view must, raise the
banner of faith in man.

THE *GOLAH*: THE NEUROTIC SOLUTION

The historical thinking of modern Jewry, in all camps, suffers at present from the consequences of a misunderstanding of the religious-political heritage. It has rejected the earlier historical picture but has not succeeded in severing its tie with it, nor in winning for itself a realistic view of all the factors which have determined the course of Jewish history. It disregards not only the unique national character of Jewry but also— and in that it continues to pursue the path of the medieval Haskalah [enlightenment]—the uniqueness of the faith of Israel, which flows from the nation, is linked to its fate, and only from within it can once again be renewed. It does not try to explain the present situation historically but to defend it from a particular point of view. Ancient and medieval apologetics sprang from the need to explain phenomena for which a causal explanation could not be found and which mortal men could not alter. In the modern world there is

*no place for apologetics; defects and difficulties
are recognized for what they are and to the extent
possible attempts are made to get at their cause
and to eliminate them. . . . All the modern explanations of* Galut *[Exile] deny the tremendously
tragic nature of the situation as well as the religious force of the ancient ideas associated with
it. The contemporary Jew of whatever religious
current cannot pretend that he is capable of bearing the many thousands of years' burden with the
same meaning it had for his forebears; or that the
external and internal conditions for a fate imbued
with such significance still exist. The* Galut *has
returned to its point of departure. It has once
again become and will continue to be what it
always has been: political subjugation that cannot
be undone except by altogether eliminating it.*

Yitzhak Baer, *Galut*

The question of the *Golah* (Exile) is the most important
and profound question a Jew must pose to himself when
trying to probe the essence of the Jewish people. The
Golah is the source of the problems the Jewish people have
been struggling with for many generations, and especially
during the last hundred years. The *Golah* is also at the very
heart of practical problems that the State of Israel is struggling with at present. Understanding of the phenomenon of
galut, of exile and diaspora, is the key to an understanding
of the Jewish people and, above all, may help us arrive at

the most reliable diagnosis of several menacing conflicts in which the Jews as a people have been and still are embroiled.

Among the Jews can be found a rich panoply of, at times, even contradictory beliefs and views, ideas and values. Some of these have been part of the people's heritage for a long time and for that reason have received greater stress. As a rule almost any conception can be backed up by a Midrash or a verse from the sources, and an altogether different view, also supported by the sources, can be set against it. However, all the interpreters of the values of Judaism will in the final analysis admit to a number of broad axioms, such as love for the Land of Israel and the Jewish people, belief in the people's right to exist, its unity, and other similarly banal and obvious principles. These do not help us arrive at a fuller understanding of the essence of the Jewish people. Only when we try to analyze *Golah* existence, which has been part of Jewish history for some twenty-five hundred years, do we approach a more substantial understanding, do we touch upon the central nerve of the Jewish problem.

In the past fifteen years attention has for the most part been focused on the practical questions raised by the *Golah*. How can the bond between the State of Israel and the *Golah* be strengthened? How can assimilation be curtailed? Will Israel become the center of the Jewish world? But the number one question that Zionism posed in all its starkness—Why *Golah* at all?—this, it seems, people are embarrassed to ask today.

There are two basic attitudes toward the *Golah*. One conception regards it as an accident that befell the Jewish people, a disaster brought down upon us by other peoples. While other peoples would have totally crumbled under such a calamity, would have lost their identity as a people, the Jewish people (because of its inner spiritual fortitude) endured and succeeded in riding out the waves of history. True, the *Golah* has been long-lasting and the Jews have not perhaps done all they could to extricate themselves from it, but nevertheless it was always regarded as a temporary situation. The nation never lost its desire to return to its land, there to reestablish its independence, there to win its national and spiritual redemption. The nation is merely awaiting more favorable conditions to clear the way for the coming of Redemption. Its path leads to Eretz Israel. When peace comes, when the situation improves, the *Golah* will dissolve and the nation will slowly stream to Israel.

This conception, which assumes that the *Golah* has been imposed on us, ignores one fundamental fact: the *Golah* was *not* imposed on us. We foisted it upon ourselves. It should be regarded not as an accident or misfortune but as a deep-reaching national perversion. That is why the way to a solution—if a solution is really desired—is altogether different from what is commonly thought. The Jewish people does not deserve praise for having endured the *Golah*. If it truly was a disaster that befell us, there would be reason to laud the Jewish people for having endured as a people. But since the Jewish people has chosen this mode of existence, and still chooses it, why be amazed that it has adapted its national being to this situation?

A second set of views regards the *Golah* as a permanent, almost natural feature of the Jewish people. It is cognizant of the close collaboration between the Jewish people and this mode of existence. In this view, the Jews are a diaspora people, and that is their existential strength. (Accepting this conception, one might wonder why other peoples do not maintain a sizable diaspora as a sure way to guarantee their national existence for thousands of years.)

This view intuitively grasps the depths of the Jewish people's need for the *Golah*, how organically it is intertwined with the Jewish essence and Jewish spiritual creativity, and therefore tries to regard the *Golah* as legitimate and normal. The question this conception sometimes raises is "Why have a state?" and even if the need for an independent national center is acknowledged today, in this view there is a duality, each pole of which is of equal worth: *Golah* and center.

This conception disregards the plain fact that the *Golah* was the source of the long chain of disasters and hardships that befell the Jewish people, that because of it a third of the Jewish people was wiped out in this generation, that in the *Golah* the Jewish people lost millions of its members by way of assimilation. On the eve of the destruction of the Second Temple the Jewish people numbered between 4 and 6 million (a respectable number indeed in the world of antiquity); because of the realities of our life in the *Golah*, at the beginning of the seventeenth century we numbered no more than 1 million. Many Jews were killed in the *Golah*, and the danger to Jewish communities there (e.g., in the Soviet Union and in South America) has not yet passed. The *Golah* is the direct cause of that bitter and cruel "Jewish fate" that has been raised almost to the status of an objective datum in all discussions of the problems of the Jews.

The simple sentence "The *Golah* is the reason for the Holocaust" is not usually uttered by Jews. The Jewish people can be likened to a person walking down the middle of a road who, when he is struck by a car driven by a madman, naturally blames only the driver and continues to walk "bravely" down the middle of the road, in the meantime trying to elaborate theories and ideologies about how the drivers have to pass him on the left and on the right so as not to hit him. This position, which views the *Golah* as a natural and legitimate mode of existence for the Jewish people, ignores the fact that the Jewish people never accorded this mode of existence ultimate spiritual legitimation.

Criticism must therefore begin by toppling these two positions and by trying to build a new synthesis. I will divide my remarks into three sections:

1. A brief historical review to prove the thesis that the *Golah* is a product of the people's will, that the Jews were not cast into Exile but cast themselves, and continue to cast themselves, into it.

2. An attempt to clarify the reasons for this phenomenon, considering that the *Golah* was the source of so many calamities for us, and that even in relatively calm periods it is considered a curse of sorts, a temporary state. I will try to shed light on the inner reasons for this love-hate relationship with the *Golah,* for this self-rape.

3. The short- and long-range practical and ideological conclusions deriving from this analysis.

THE *GOLAH* AS WILLED

I will begin by noting some simple, well-known historical facts, which when brought together are enlightening, at times even disconcerting.

Abraham, the father of the nation, was not born in Eretz Israel. He was called upon by God to leave his homeland and his father's house and to go forth to a new land chosen by God in order to found there a new people by a new cov-

enant. The first Jew was thus the first *oleh,* the first immigrant to Eretz Israel. But he was also the first *yored,* the
first emigrant from the country. The economic situation in
Eretz Israel was difficult, and Abraham immediately set
out for Egypt. How amazing to think that this old man,
who on God's command left the land of his birth and the
home of his father for the promised land which was to be
the land of the nation to be born of his seed, that this
wealthy man does not manage to stay on there but instead
leaves it for another land! His weakness could be more
readily understood had he been overcome by longing for
the land of his birth. But that is not what happened. He
does not return to his native land but goes to another land.
The concept *yored,* one who leaves, goes down from, Eretz
Israel, was born in the story of Abraham. The first Jew is
both the first *oleh,* the first to go up to the land of Israel,
and the first *yored,* the first to descend. The Jew bears
within himself these two essences of "ascent" and "de-
scent," of *aliyah* and *yeridah,* throughout all of history.
Abraham ascends, descends, and once again ascends. No
more than two generations pass and Jacob, the grandson,
again goes down to Egypt. He, however, does not return,
does not go up again, but dies in the *Golah.* He followed
his sons to the *Golah,* for there was famine in the land. I
am certain that other inhabitants of the land stayed on despite the famine. Jacob, however, requests that his bones
be brought back to Eretz Israel and be buried there. Is that
the secret destiny of the land, to be a burial ground for
Jewish bones, or is it also a land of life? We will return to
that question, but here let us take note: the patriarchs, a
new nation being born, and the attitude to the land, which
in a certain sense should have served as a model for the nation as a whole, are already ambivalent.

The Jewish people was created in the Golah. Do we

grasp the full significance of this? The Jewish people was not born in its land. The elementary primal tie between a people and its homeland is for us not natural. Our nationhood was forged in the *Golah,* and the *Golah* as the crucible of our birth has penetrated to the very cells of our being. Moreover, the Torah was given to this people, not in Eretz Israel, but in the desert. The Torah—the system of values that were to define our identity and determine our purpose—was not given in Eretz Israel. The special bond between the people and God has its beginnings in the desert, in no-man's-land, in the intermediate region between the *Golah* and Eretz Israel. We will see how throughout its history the nation always searches for this no-man's-land, especially when it seeks an answer or spiritual renewal. In the desert we are in a state of death-life. The desert is a place of death, and in that place of death the young nation is spiritually revitalized. The desert is also a sterile place, untouched, pure, and there the nation makes its preparations to enter the land. And God demands the most punctilious preparations. The entry into the land has tremendous significance. It is not only the physical conquest of the land by a nation of nomads, it is also a conquest imbued with spiritual significance. Stringent conditions are laid down together with the promise of the land, for might alone cannot assure retention of it. The nation can maintain its hold on the land only if it pays heed to the voice of God and observes His commandments. If it does not meet these conditions it will be subject to the harshest punishments, the ultimate of which is expulsion from the land, Exile. The land is conceived of as sacred; the sins of the nation will defile it and then the land will vomit up the people from it. In these early texts the fundamental principle is already established: *the people takes precedence over the land in every sense.* There are harsh and clear conditions to remain in the land, but there are no conditions pertaining to the very existence of the people. The people can sin abominably, and still its existence is assured beyond all doubt. It will be punished but not annihilated. It will go into exile, but exile is not the end; it is possible to live in exile and possible to return from it. It was already impressed on the early consciousness of the people that exile is caused not by some external force but by the people's own inner spiritual transgression.

While the people is still in the desert, before it has enjoyed even a minute of independence, before it has set foot on its land, heaven has already indicated the possibility of going into exile and returning from it. The nation born in the *Golah* gets a clear inkling of the very real possibility of a national existence without a land, without a territory. (It is doubtful that other peoples could even imagine such a possibility.)

The desert experience is etched deeply in the consciousness of the people. All the national-religious holidays we celebrate—Sukkoth, Passover, Shavuoth—as distinct from the purely religious holidays, such as Rosh Hashanah and Yom Kippur, are associated with the people's existence in the desert.

The nation is therefore afraid to enter the land. And the word *fear* is the key to understanding the people's relationship to Eretz Israel. The nation fears that it will not be able to live up to the difficult conditions God places on its existence in the land. The story of the scouts is very apposite here. The nation that has already successfully fought other peoples since its departure from Egypt is overwhelmed by fear of the inhabitants of the land, so much so that it wants to return to Egypt. An entire generation has to die in the desert and a new generation that had no experience of the *Golah* has to be born for the people to be worthy and made ready to enter the land.

The nation reaches the land, conquers it, and sets up its kingdom, and after some time the kingdom is split. Centuries pass and the Kingdom of Israel is destroyed, the ten tribes are exiled and disappear. This, the "Israeli" part of the nation, apparently always acted more naturally and normally than did the "Judean-Jewish" part that lived in Judea, and also behaved normally when it was cast into exile. When it lost its land and patrimony, it also lost its identity and nationhood. From the beginning of history this segment of the Jewish people already acted as other nations do.

One hundred fifty years later the Kingdom of Judea is destroyed, the people are exiled to Babylonia, and endure. The nation preserves its identity and demonstrates that a nation *can* preserve its identity without physically holding on to the land. It reveals the strength of holding on in imagination and spirit. This exile is very short-lived, no more than fifty years. In 520 B.C.E., when Cyrus' proclamation permits the nation to return to the land to reestablish its independence there, only *part* of the nation returns to build the Second Temple; a sizable and important part of the nation does not return but remains in the first exile *of its own free will*. People who were born in Eretz Israel, or whose fathers were born there, refuse to return to it and prefer to remain in the *Golah*. They do not deny their origin and national identity—on the contrary, their attachment to the nation remains profound. They even support and encourage those who do return, but they themselves do not join them. Here we find the first point confirming our assumption about the source of the *Golah*, which henceforth comes to dominate Jewish history. In Song of Songs Rabbah (8:9) it is written: "If only Israel had gone up in its entirety from the *Golah,* the Second Temple would not have been destroyed."

A great truth is contained in this statement. That segment of the people which does not join the repatriates reestablishing independence sows the seeds of calamity. Perhaps it already foresees that this national center may not endure and that therefore it is better to let the land remain a dream, a goal and object of longing, than to see it as a disappointing reality.

On the eve of the destruction of the Second Temple about half of the Jewish people were already scattered among lands other than Eretz Israel. The Jewish people left its land of its own will and dispersed among various and odd lands. We have evidence of the existence of Jewish communities north of Odessa in Russia, on the Libyan border, in Babylonia, Alexandria, and Asia Minor. The Jews settled in distant places of their own free will, not because there was not room enough in Eretz Israel. The indisputable fact is that the land is filled with alien peoples; they live there, settle on parts of it, because Jews do not live there. These diasporas maintain a profound attachment to Eretz Israel, contribute to the Temple, and even give political support to the rebellion against Rome, that insane and hopeless rebellion which brought about the destruction of the land and the destruction of Jerusalem. This unnecessary rebellion, the most radical of all the revolts against the Roman Empire, led by religious-national fanatics who dragged the entire nation into a futile struggle—this rebellion is even somewhat encouraged by the Jews of the Diaspora. They who live in a distinctly Gentile environment, among idols and fetishes, in the very heart of "defilement," they who freely decided to forgo the slightest shadow of national life in their land, encourage the extremists and fanatics in Jerusalem to demand the removal of the statue from the Temple in order to express full political and religious independence, something not granted any people in the Roman Empire. (I will soon come to internal reasons leading to this futile revolt.)

Rabban Johanan Ben-Zakkai, in departing from Jerusalem shortly before the destruction of the Temple to establish the academy of Jabneh, already knew of the impending destruction and was aware of the need to give up the land as a principal component of the national identity. His move was preparatory to the creation of an utterly exilic existence in which even the *Golah*-center polarity would cease to function. The new Torah erected is actually a return of sorts to the desert situation. That is to say, the people that twice failed in independence and again lost its land is once again making preparations to return to it. But this time the preparations will be serious, and in a certain sense perhaps even endless: full redemption, the end of history, the end of days.

Thus begin eighteen hundred years of Exile, and I think I will not be terribly mistaken if I assert that in all these centuries, from the destruction of the Second Temple to the beginning of Zionism, and in fact right up to the present, the people has not made a serious effort to return to Eretz Israel, not only to reestablish its political independence but even to try to settle there. This people, which displayed resourcefulness, flexibility, and cunning intelligence in reaching almost every point on the globe—from the Atlas Mountains to the steppes of China, from Tierra del Fuego in South America to the Siberian wastes—made no real attempt to return to and settle in Eretz Israel. The Jews wandered constantly from place to place, changed countries, but passed Eretz Israel by. The Jews settled in numbers in all lands of the Mediterranean basin, except for Eretz Israel. In their wanderings the Jews circled near the country, were drawn to it, but also feared and avoided it. As a result of the expulsion from Spain at the end of the Middle Ages many thousands of Jews were dispersed throughout the lands of the East, but only a handful reached Eretz Israel. Jews lived in Syria, Egypt, Iraq, Yemen, Greece, and Turkey; only Eretz Israel was without Jews. The greatest of Jewish philosophers, Maimonides, resided in Egypt, a short distance from Eretz Israel, and when Saladin conquered Jerusalem in 1187, Maimonides noted this momentous event in his writings by not so much as a word. It is depressing to hear all those ideologues who enthusiastically count the number of Jews in Eretz Israel in each century in order to prove the continuity of a Jewish presence there, who laud the family that maintained a continuous presence in the Galilee town of Peki'in, and who are driven to extremes of joy by every rabbi who came to the country with his followers and managed to stay here for a couple of years. If the Jews had been attached to Eretz Israel as they were attached to Poland, for example, or Babylon, and if the Jews had fought for their right to live in Eretz Israel as they fought for their right to live in England, from which they were expelled in 1290, there would be no pathetic need to prove that some Jews did live here and that Rabbi Judah Halevi was overcome by longing and despite everything came here. All those small groups of Jews who did come here —and there was always a trickle of immigration of this sort—demonstrate that it was indeed possible to reach the country and to settle here, but that most of the people did not want to do so. True, restrictions and harsh decrees were imposed on the Jews here, but where were there no restrictions, prohibitions, expulsions, pogroms, and harsh decrees? The Jews managed to make their way through fissures in the walls around many countries, endured all kinds of regimes, lived in foreign and remote cultures. They could have done the same in Eretz Israel, where since the Destruction the regime changed hands six times. The conclusive evidence that the Jews made no effort to return to Eretz Israel is the number of Jews in the country at the beginning of the nineteenth century: after all the many "immigrations" no more than 5,000 Jews (of a nation numbering 2.5 million) lived here. In Yemen, where the Jews suffered harsh repression, where they lived in a cultural and physical wasteland, there alone at that time, the beginning of the nineteenth century, lived some 30,000 Jews.

Zionism emerged at the end of the last century not from renewed longings for Eretz Israel, nor from sudden abhorrence of Exile. The Jews always hated the *Golah* and longed with all their soul for Eretz Israel! But the hatred of Exile and the longings for Eretz Israel did not budge the Jews. Zionism began with a fear of the *Golah*. How dangerous and terrible this existence could be suddenly became clear to the Jews. And among a few the fear of the *Golah* overcame the fear of Eretz Israel.

At its inception Zionism was a movement of a few isolated individuals. It was rejected by most of the people: above all, the religious Jews, but also by the Bund, the Jewish socialists, by assimilationists of all colors, and by those who dreamed of cultural autonomy. The mass of the people did not want Zionism and did not believe in it. This decisive fact must not be allowed to be forgotten. After the Balfour Declaration was issued and the gates of Eretz Israel were opened, and a great power such as Great Britain supported the possibility of establishing a Jewish state in Eretz Israel, the Jewish people still did not come. Not even the cleverest sophistry can blot out this decisive fact, which had such terrible consequences. The Jewish people could have established a Jewish state in Eretz Israel in the twenties. Of the millions of Jews who emigrated from the East to the West, only 30,000 reached Eretz Israel between 1917 and 1921. In the entire decade of the twenties hardly 100,000 Jews reached Eretz Israel. In that period the Jewish people numbered about 15 million. Had only 10 percent of the Jewish people arrived here, even only 5 percent, a Jewish state might have been established before the Holocaust—on all the territory of Eretz Israel or on part of it. A million Jews in Eretz Israel in the twenties would have been a fact of no mean importance in the slowly awakening East. The Holocaust itself would never have reached its terrible dimensions had a Jewish state been established before World War II. The Jewish people, itself, therefore bears indirect responsibility for its horrendous fate in this century.

But if someone still needs final and irrefutable proof of the Jewish people's dubious attitude to Eretz Israel, of the fact that it did not make a serious attempt to return to its land, of its fear of return and its stubborn clinging to the *Golah,* all he needs do is take a look at the thirty years of the Jewish state's existence. The gates are open, the possibilities great—but the *olim* do not come. The waves of immigration that arrived here were comprised for the most part of people fleeing distress: refugees of the Holocaust, refugees from the Arab countries, refugees from communist countries, and so on. Only an insignificant minority came to Israel of its own free will, and this minority again proves, paradoxically, as did the small immigrations of earlier centuries, that it is also possible to come to Israel as a matter of free choice.

The common factor in the non-coming to Israel of the Jewish communities, which differ among themselves sociologically, is the same as that which kept Jews from coming here over the centuries. Russian Jews who endanger their lives to leave the Soviet Union prefer to live in some German suburb and subsist on the welfare handouts of a Jewish or Christian organization rather than come to Israel, which offers what can assuredly be considered reasonable conditions of absorption. Until recently, Lebanese Jews preferred to live a hundred yards from the headquarters of the Popular Front for the Liberation of Palestine, in closest proximity to the greatest centers of anti-Israel hatred and enmity, rather than come to Israel. The Jews of Argentina will prefer to live in a fascist country with a deteriorating economy and a rising tide of anti-Semitism, rather than come to Israel.

· The examples multiply: the Jews of Syria until 1967, the Jews of Algiers, the Jews of Iran, and, of course, all of Western Jewry. Each community has, it seems, its own explanation for the absence of immigration to Israel from it: here the explanation is economic, there a matter of security, here the difficulties of uprooting, there religious. But precisely because the explanations are so varied, and at times contradict one another, and considering that Israel has changed so much in the last thirty years—from a pioneering to a capitalistic country, from a primarily secular country to one with a religious-national accent—a deeplying fundamental explanation must be found for this clinging to the *Golah*. It is inconceivable that such varied factors always lead to the very same phenomenon.

If, for example, we were to bring together typical representatives of the different groups that make up the Jewish community—a Satamar hasid and a Lubavitcher hasid, an Orthodox rabbi, a Conservative rabbi, a Reform rabbi, a Zionist leader, a community worker, a professor who identifies as a Jew and a professor who has assimilated, a rich Jew and a poor Jew, a student belonging to the Jewish

Defense League and a leftist student—we would discover
that each of them interprets Jewishness and his identification with it differently, each of them envisages Israel and
its mission differently. Each of them has an altogether
different reason for not coming to live in Israel, and each
has a different critique of what is going on in Israel. But
one thing they all share: they do not come to settle in Israel.

Jews from all periods of history, from remote places and
different civilizations, could be added to this gathering.
Each would bring with him his period's view of Judaism,
his emphases and interpretations, and again, with all the
vast differences, one thing would be shared by them all:
their not coming to Israel.

For a phenomenon of such long duration as the Exile, for
so many variations of Jewish existence, partial explanations relevant only to their time will not do. The primary,
basic reasons for this phenomenon must be sought out, especially in light of the critical fact that in all its spiritual
and existential expressions the Jewish people rejected the
Golah as a permanent option for Jewish existence and
deeply negated it. Judaism never accorded the *Golah* legitimation. Quite the contrary. The *Golah* was always regarded as a disaster, a calamity, a curse, a fall, the root of
all ill, and certainly as a temporary situation. The *She-
khinah* itself went into exile with the people. The world will
not be set right until the people has returned to its land.

This was not only an abstract idea, it was a living existential position. From morning to night the Jews thought of
Eretz Israel and prayed toward it, spoke of returning to the
land, and pined for it. The liturgical poetry of redemption
was part of the being of the religious Jew (and up until the
mid-nineteenth century what Jew was not a religious

Jew?). "Next year in Jerusalem" was a fundamental component of the Jewish spiritual consciousness. The belief that the dead would roll underground to the Holy Land on the day of Resurrection is an indication of how deeply embedded was the conception of the transitory nature of the *Golah*. According to this belief, even if a Jew died in the *Golah* his corpse would undergo the hardships of rolling through caverns to return to Eretz Israel. The Resurrection would take place in Eretz Israel. From morning to night the Jews studied the commandments associated with Eretz Israel and celebrated holidays according to a liturgical calendar that corresponded to the seasons there. The messianic movements that burst onto the Jewish scene and the tremendous resonance they had among the people clearly reveal the depths of the desire for redemption shared by all parts of the nation.

What we see, then, is on the one hand hatred and total rejection of the situation of Exile, and on the other hand a powerful drive to maintain it and live in it. All the attempts (and they were few) to grant legitimation to the *Golah* experience have failed. That includes the attempt by Reform Jewry in the United States to establish the legitimacy of the Jew's existence in the land where he lives, replacing the national component of his bond to Eretz Israel with a kind of disembodied link like that of the Roman Catholic to the Vatican. The Reform Jews failed in this even though, at least theoretically, they had all the conditions for success. After World War II they returned to the fold of the Zionist movement.

What reveals itself here is behavior of a clearly neurotic sort: the nation hates the *Golah* and dreams of Eretz Israel, the nation rejects Exile at all levels of its authentic spiritual activity, but at the same time all its historical activity is preoccupied with one end: how to endure in Exile, how to continue to maintain this hated existence.

What explanations have the Jews themselves proffered for this situation? The principal reason they latch on to is associated with the term *the fleshpots:* that is to say, the fear of economic difficulties in Eretz Israel, or the fear of having to give up a sound economic position in the lands of the *Golah.*

But is that really so? I know of no explanation more misleading than this one which has been offered up as incontestable truth.

I maintain that it is impossible to explain the history of any people solely in terms of economic dynamics and motivation, and to try to do so for the Jews is to court especial difficulty. We must bare the cause of the Jews' need to remain in the *Golah,* a need that brought them so much disaster. Not only must this cause be clearly established, its characteristic force among the Jewish people must also be explained, especially since other peoples seem free of this need. Must we really agree with Marx that the only true god of the Jews is Mammon, that the driving motive of the Jews is the lust for lucre? That only thus can we explain the profound pathological attraction of the people for a form of existence it itself so thoroughly impugns?

To claim that money is the sole driving force of Jewish history? Even the most brutal anti-Semite would, I think, hesitate before making such a claim. On the one hand we see the Jews giving up their lives to sanctify God's name, accepting the harshest decrees rather than be disloyal to an idea and belief, and on the other hand those same Jews are described as being motivated solely by money. How totally absurd!

There is, however, still the question of fact. Did the

Golah actually create congenial economic situations for the
Jews? Did the Jews (said to be motivated only by greed)
actually attain what they sought by residing in the *Golah?*
The answer, it seems, is quite irrefutable. Throughout their
history in the *Golah* the Jews did not even come near to attaining high economic status. The vast majority were mis-
erably poor. Living in the *Golah,* they were subject to the
severest economic restrictions; their property was constantly whittled away. What were the economic achievements of the Jews of Poland or of Yemen, or of the cave
dwellers of the Atlas Mountains in Morocco?

Moreover, living in Eretz Israel did not necessitate an
immediate and sharp drop in economic status. Would a
wealthy Jewish merchant in Syria or Iraq have lost all his
capital by moving his home to Eretz Israel? What justification is there for imagining that in their relationship to
money the Jews are essentially different from all other peoples, and that that is why they clung to the *Golah* at such a
costly historical price—especially when there is no proof
that life in the *Golah* provided the Jews with economic security?

The use of the biblical term *fleshpots* is curious. It origi-
nates in the desert generation, and we know quite well that
the people of that generation had been slaves in Egypt and
therefore had no "fleshpots" to return to. Longing for
them, they longed for something they never had. That we
persist in using this term, itself totally baseless, is an indication of how paradoxical is use of this coinage and of how
little it reflects the real reason for the attraction to the
Golah. The economic explanation is a camouflage or substitute for much deeper reasons, admission to which is
feared.

Neither is the "security" argument, according to which
Eretz Israel is a dangerous place that "devours its inhabit-

ants," any more convincing. In all periods of the Exile we
find Jews living in the most dangerous places, under the
cruelest rulers. We ourselves have witnessed how the Jews
of Iran, who could have left their country and become citizens of Israel within three hours, did not fear as dangerous
and mad a ruler as the Ayatollah Khomeini and remained
instead on the slopes of the erupting Iranian volcano. Life
in Eretz Israel was no more dangerous than life anywhere
else, and in a certain sense was less dangerous than in
many other places. Had the Jews settled in Eretz Israel
even as a territorial minority, they would have had many
more rights than as an alien minority dispersed in many
places.

The "war situation in the country" will prove itself a hol-
low reason once peace is achieved. We know full well that
peace will not bring waves of immigration to these shores.

Two convenient anti-Semitic myths that we have
adopted—the myth of Jewish greed and the myth of Jewish
cowardice—are thus refuted. For if the Jews really were
money lovers and cowards, it is likely that they would have
long since come to live in their country, thereby sparing
themselves much suffering and misfortune.

AN INTERIM SUMMING UP

I have so far tried to prove three theses.

1. The *Golah* as situation and possibility is one of the
most fundamental components of the essence of the Jewish
people. It is found in the atoms and molecules that make
up our spiritual and existential identity. It is an organic
part of our national mythos. It is not an externally imposed
situation but an internal situation chosen by the people and

desired by it. Religiously, and I would add nationally, the people's existence is unconditional. The people can commit the most horrible abominations in God's sight, it can lose all signs of its national identity, and still its existence is assured. *It will be punished but will never be annihilated.* By contrast, sovereign existence in Eretz Israel, and even living in Eretz Israel, is hedged with very difficult, and not altogether understood, conditions. Outside of its land the nation can maintain a temporary and humiliating existence, but that is still existence. There are very few peoples who can conceive of a national identity being preserved when the entire nation is exiled from its homeland.

2. In all of the nation's spiritual activity throughout history, the *Golah* was deemed a humiliating and lowly experience, a fallen state. The *Golah* was never accorded legitimation as a *permanent* situation. The question was always how to endure in the *Golah* until the coming of redemption, a hope never abandoned by the people. Redemption was not abstract but meant actual physical return to Eretz Israel. The *Golah* was considered a situation leading the nation into duplicity. (Abraham, the first exile, arrives in Egypt and is immediately forced to lie about his wife.) Lie and redemption intermesh, for the nation must tread a cautious path around dual loyalties, it must masquerade as nationally dead so as not to set its nationhood in overt conflict with the nationhood of the people among whom it lives. But the nation's existence is unconditioned, and hence it exercises all its imaginative powers and invests all its existential energies in order to endure the *Golah*, although spiritually it rejects it.

In this way a paradoxical, almost pathological, situation is created. The nation is drawn to the *Golah* as a possibility inherent in its being, it abhors it, does all it can to endure within it, but by its steadily improving ability to live in the

Golah it constantly pushes the return to its land further into the future. The people feels guilty for not returning to its land, and therefore extols and exalts it more and more, infuses it with a profound and sacred essence, makes it wonderful, all to justify its own unworthiness to return. On the other hand, it describes the land as a nightmare, dangerous, predatory, "devouring its inhabitants," in order to justify its fear of return.

3. I tried to demonstrate that the "fleshpots," the fear of the land's desolateness, the fear of physical danger, and the like are superficial excuses, and that it can be shown that entire large Jewish communities lived in conditions of poverty and danger, in the desolate lands of other peoples, and were not at all deterred by this existence. Moreover, the Jews were the great wanderers of history, passing from one land to another, but in their wanderings passed Eretz Israel by. Religious Jews did not return because they feared to "anticipate the coming of the Messiah," and secular Jews did not return because they had a spiritual "message" for the Gentiles. The wealthy feared for their property and the poor feared separation from their near ones. The socialists hoped to abolish all national barriers, and the Jews who lived in Afghanistan or India simply did not know where Eretz Israel was (although they knew where England and France were). The Jews who lived in Rome feared the harsh Roman rule in Eretz Israel, and the Jews who lived in Syria or Egypt waited for the land to fill up with other Jews so that they could come as last in line. Reform Jews do not come to live in Israel because Reform Judaism is not accorded full recognition, and Orthodox Jews do not come because the Sabbath is desecrated in Tel Aviv. I am convinced that in the twenty-first or twenty-second century there will be colonies in space and among these colonies there will also be a small Jewish community, with a rabbi

and small synagogue suspended in space in which the tal-
ented Jewish scientists will pray "Next year in Jerusalem."
I am sure that some of them will send their children for a
year of study in Israel, and who knows, perhaps there will
be an Israeli *shaliach* (emissary) in the community center
trying to encourage *aliyah* (immigration) to Israel. And
when he is asked why the Jews are not coming he will try
to explain the difficulties of adjusting to the forces of grav-
ity in Israel. There is no limit to the imagination's ability to
find excuses. But where is the truth to be found?

And so we come back to the fundamental question:
Why? What is the reason for the painful obsessional opting
for Exile? Why do the Jews have such a fear of normal,
sovereign life in their own country? That, I believe, is the
number one question of the Jewish people, deserving of all
our spiritual energies. Here I will try to propose several answers, which are still no more than speculations, working
hypotheses.

THE *GOLAH* AS SOLUTION TO THE CONFLICT BETWEEN RELIGION AND NATIONALITY

The Jewish people presents a quite interesting and unusual
blend of nationality and religion. On one side is a natural
system (family, tribe, nation) and on the other a spiritual,
a system of values expressed primarily in the Jewish religion. The system of nationality is wide-flung and most flex-
ible. The definition of a Jew as the child of a Jewish
mother (the earliest of definitions) draws the nationality
boundaries to the most indistinct limit. Belonging to the
Jewish people by virtue of this definition does not oblige a
Jew to live in a specific territory, to speak a specific lan-

guage, to adopt specific cultural and spiritual values, or to manifest loyalty to a specific group of individuals or to a binding national framework. His biological affiliation suffices to identify him as a Jew.

At the same time, a distinct system of values, defined and demarcated by thousands of precise details of daily behavior, attaches to this national definition (but remains outside the definition!). These values and the way of life they describe are not binding in terms of the definition; however, a spiritual claim is made for them. These two systems, of course, intermesh, but not to the point that they are indistinguishable.

Every people has distinctly national elements such as a territory, a language, a national framework (a state or tribal framework), as well as spiritual-religious elements such as a system of culture, values, and way of life. But the balance between these two sets of elements is tipped to the national side. The Chinese people, which has been in existence for some five thousand years, identifies itself first and foremost in terms of the national elements of territory, language, and national framework, and not on the basis of a set of behavioral, cultural, or religious values, elements which in the course of the generations have undergone far-reaching change (from Confucius to Mao, from Buddhism to communism, and so on.

Precisely because the Jewish religious identity was so specific and so rigorously defined, the national identity could be so vague. For example, since Yom Kippur, a day with very distinct meanings and content, is supposed to unite all the Jews, the Jews observing it can be remote from one another, scattered over many lands, can speak different languages and live in different national landscapes and situations. The strength of the religious-spiritual base made a most feeble national existence possible. On the other hand, let us not forget that nationality sets limits on the religion. The religious contents are not intended to make the whole world Jewish; they are intended only for the nation. That is to say, the Jewish message was restricted by a definition of a national character (child of a Jewish mother) and not by a definition of a religious nature (belief in God or in Moses or in the Torah). What this means is that the religion legitimizes the Jew's identity, even if he maintains no ties with it. The religion provides legitimation for the faintest identity. A Jew can be totally assimilated (and in the view of some even an apostate), with no national tie whatsoever to the people, and the religious system will identify him as a Jew with a religious potential, even a candidate for repentance and return. Were the Jewish people to identify itself only as a national entity, it never would have been able to endure such a frail definition.

There is permanent tension between the national and religious systems, stemming from the constant contradiction between their goals. Here is a normal system functioning in accord with the basic needs of national existence within a specified territory, and here is a spiritual system setting spiritual goals for the people and trying to make its existence subject to religious-spiritual demands. These are two different codes.

The contradiction between these two systems constantly feeds a number of serious conflicts in Jewish history, beginning with the conflict between Moses and segments of the nation, between priest and king, and between prophet and king. Samuel, for example, at first refuses to anoint a king over Israel, regarding this as a betrayal of himself and his mission. The prophets are always on the kings' heels, sharply criticizing them for the way they rule and intervening in general political and state questions. They are

unable to accept a natural national dynamic that follows
the course of plain national interest. That they see as betrayal and denial of the calling to be a "kingdom of priests
and a holy people." True, struggle between the national regime and the religious system has occurred in many countries. It is not unique to the Jews. Among us, however,
these struggles took an especially sharp turn because the
national system was fundamentally the weaker of the two
and because the religion's arena of struggle was restricted
solely to the Jewish people. The decisive fact, that the national systems of other peoples were immeasurably more
powerful than that of Israel, becomes even more apparent
when it is noted that many peoples changed their religions
and replaced their spiritual systems according to national
needs, whereas among the Jewish people the national system could never triumph over the religious. What is more,
the other great monotheistic religions broke through the
national boundary and found other outlets for the energies
of the conflict. When they realized that they could not impose themselves on the national regime, they went out to
spread their message among other peoples. The Church-
state conflict at the end of the Middle Ages, which ended
in the victory of the state, led the Christian religion to
launch a new campaign of missionary conquest. Instead of
fighting within the national arena until blood was drawn,
the religious-spiritual energy found a new channel in its
struggle against the "infidels." The religious systems of
other peoples always find indirect ways of waging ideological warfare. The universal essence of Christianity and
Islam, even of the great Eastern religions, frees them from
having to enter into a total confrontation with a specific
national regime. The Jewish religion, by contrast, does not
have such outlets; it has no universal intention. It is meant
solely for the Jewish people and has no interest in other

peoples. A person wanting to become part of Judaism must first of all join the Jewish people. The Jewish religion cannot concede or compromise its rule of the Jewish people. The success or failure of the religion can be judged only in a Jewish context. For that reason, the religion's interference in the totality of Jewish life is unavoidable and of the essence.

The constant conflict between the religious and national systems always inflames the people and is liable to tear it asunder. All the other conflicts—class, economic, political —are dwarfed in comparison with this conflict, which actually came to an explosive head on the eve of the destruction of the Second Temple. Nationally, this hopeless revolt was totally unnecessary, but it was necessary religiously, to protect Jewish religious identity from the "idol in the Temple." The strength of Jewish religious consciousness is what dragged the people into a revolt unparalleled anywhere in the entire Roman Empire in its extremism. The revolt and the destruction that came in its wake were for many long years a national trauma. The conflict between the national and religious codes had again been bared in historical reality.

The nation, aware of the acute conflict it contains and aware of its dangers, protects its existence by departing for the *Golah* and by taking up residence there. The solution to the threatening conflict is—existence in Exile. Since life in the *Golah* is not life in an all-embracing total Jewish reality in which a decisive stand can be taken, the potential conflict is muted. The framework of Jewish life in the *Golah* is essentially voluntaristic. The Jews do not rule over each other. The Jew is Jewishly free and determines the intensity of his Jewishness as he wishes. The ability to coerce is limited. One small step and he is outside the most rigid ghetto. The Jew can be requested and called upon to comply with the religion's commandments, but he cannot be *compelled* to do so. At most he can be outcast, in the most extreme cases excommunicated, but he cannot be killed.

In the *Golah* the center of conflict is deflected from inside to outside. The people are constantly assailed by the non-Jewish external environment. Of supreme importance is the preservation of existence itself, and all are united around that objective. Debates about the substance of identity assume secondary importance, never reaching the point of physical war. Whereas other nations have waged real civil war, with real weapons in hand, for real war objectives—such as control of properties and of centers of political power—and one or another position could be fully imposed, among us the contending parties were at the mercy of a third party, alien and hostile, and it always posed the real threat.

The *Golah* freed the religious and national systems from having to do battle with each other. It muted and checked the struggle. Here is an example. The Lubavitcher Rebbe living in New York can only ask and try to persuade the Jews of New York not to travel on the Sabbath, to send their children to Jewish schools, to eat kosher meat, and the like. But should he come to Israel he would be able, and it would be his religious duty, to compel the Jews not to travel on the Sabbath, to educate their children religiously, to eat kosher. The national framework makes coercion obligatory because it makes it possible. In New York he is unable to enter into a real conflict with other Jews over matters of Jewish substance and content because the framework of *Golah* existence does not allow for real conflict. At most it allows for spiritual-intellectual conflict (and even that often of an altogether mild sort, because what is required is to maintain Jewish identity itself, for it is constantly at the front line of attack). But a clear-cut resolution of the issue is possible in a total Jewish reality, just as a clear decision on issues of Belgian or French values is possible in a total Belgian or French reality. Hence the conflict that will erupt in full force in Israel cannot emerge in the *Golah*. (Take, for example, the radical difference between the behavior of ultra-Orthodox circles toward secular Jews in Israel and in the *Golah*.)

It is as if the nation intuitively grasps how dangerous this inner conflict is and seeks to postpone and neutralize it by avoiding the situation in which it comes fully to the fore. That is the meaning of the neurotic solution: an escape to a situation which forestalls a feared conflict.

We need speak not only of a religious-national conflict but also of a spiritual-national conflict. The secular conception tries to replace religious with other spiritual contents, such as justice, an egalitarian society, pacifism, values of study. In this regard the religious Jews are correct in arguing that there is no such thing as a secular Jew, that is, one who defines himself solely on the basis of national contents. A leftist Jew living in Paris who interprets the Jewish mission to be the creation of an exemplary egalitarian society cannot come into real conflict with other Jews over this. At most he can enter into spiritual-intellectual conflict with them. In a total Jewish reality, where a decision on equality, socialism, and the like is possible, as in any other society, that Jew must come into real violent conflict with his surroundings in order to convert his interpretation of Judaism into reality.

Again, these conflicts occur among all peoples. But because of the inherent weakness of the national element among us vis-à-vis the spiritual-religious element, the conflict among the Jews is much more severe.

THE *GOLAH* AS ANSWERING TO THE NEED TO BE A DIFFERENT PEOPLE, A CHOSEN PEOPLE

Deep among the primary strands of our identity is the demand to be different, singular, unique, set apart from the family of nations. One of the fundamental elements of the Jewish religious conception is represented in the phrase "You have chosen us." It runs like a thread through all spiritual levels of Jewish religious-national activity. "A nation that shall dwell alone and not take account of the Gentiles." A different people, altogether different. The notion of being "like all the nations" has a clearly negative ring for the Jew.

Is it, however, possible to be different from all nations? Is there any such thing as "all the nations"? On the individual level we would immediately see the absurdity of the demand to be different. If someone got up and announced that he differs from everybody else, we would tell him, yes, he differs from everybody else but so, too, everybody differs from everybody else. Each of us is different. But it is impossible to be "more different." If someone got up and declared that he feels he is different beyond the relative difference between all individuals and that his calling is to find this difference and to heighten it and under no circumstances can he be like everyone else, we would take him for a fool or a madman. This individual has the audacity and pretense to place all the billions of people in the world in one group, those who behave like all men, and himself in a separate group, different from all the others. But still, even though to insist on being chosen and different from all men seems absurd and mad on the individual plane, astonishingly enough we readily adopt this conception on the national plane. How often have I been amazed to hear not only religious but also secular Jews say: We must not be like all other nations; if the State of Israel is to be like all other states it has no right to exist. Nothing is more insulting to the Jew, and at times also to the Israeli, than to tell him that the Jewish people is a people like all others.

Does the concept "like all the nations" have any real meaning? Is it possible to place all the different national variations, all the tribes and peoples with their different customs and manifold religions, in one category and say they behave like "all the nations" and only the Jewish people is different, or should be different from them? Even if the Jewish people in Israel were to set up a purely Halachic state conducting itself in accord with nothing but Jewish law and the Torah, and all the citizens were to go about in *kapotes* and *shtreimels,* would this state differ essentially from all other countries? Would it differ from the others more than the Islamic Republic of Iran or Saudi Arabia or Nepal differ from all other countries?

Is it at all possible to be different beyond the difference obtaining among all peoples? It is only possible to be different within the range of the relative difference among all peoples, but this is never an absolute, it is only a relative difference. And all peoples partake of this relative difference. But an unequivocal demand is addressed to the Jewish people to be different from all other peoples, to be other. Mounds of interpretation have piled up on the issue of this difference. The Jewish people groaned under this inner demand, which it could not fulfill in the framework of normal sovereign life in its land, because it is simply impossible to fulfill it. The only way to meet the demand was to go into Exile. When the Jewish people is in Exile it indeed differs essentially from all other peoples.

Here is the artist's palette: red, blue, green, yellow, white, black. Each color differs from the others and is distinguished from them, but no color is "more different" than any other. If we want to separate out the color red, but are unable to change its essence, we have to change its situation among the other colors. If we take it and spread it as drops among the other colors, it will then be "more different," not in its essence but in its situation. That is the Jewish *Golah* solution.

The *Golah* creates the difference between us and other peoples. Since we are unable to set ourselves apart essentially, we set ourselves apart "technically," if such a term can be used in this context. The technical separation creates an essence which, although we are not particularly fond of it and it causes us physical and spiritual suffering, does constitute a neurotic solution to an impossible demand. The Jew's lonely existence among alien peoples, even if he resembles the people among whom he lives in every respect, speaks their languages, and participates in their life, it itself, his mere being a Jew, sets him off and provides him with the good and satisfying feeling of being different.

THE DISTURBED FATHER-MOTHER EQUILIBRIUM: A PSYCHOANALYTIC EXCURSUS

Once some scoundrels came to him and said, Dear sir, we know a short way to travel unto Eretz Israel, a way through caves and tunnels. If you so desire, come with us and we will go before you as your guides. He consented to go with

*them. And as they proceeded they came upon a
deep chasm filled with water and mud and filth.
This they crossed on a plank reaching from one
side to the other, supporting themselves with a
stick they put into the pool. And when the Baal
Shem Tov wanted to cross on it, behold he saw
the flaming sword which turned every way and
he retreated. For it would have been a great
danger for him to cross on it. And the Baal Shem
Tov said to himself, Surely, it is not for naught I
have come here. And going back he struck that
frog.*

Shivhei Ha-Besht (*Stories of the Baal Shem Tov*)

In his *History and Psychoanalysis,** Saul Friedlander
discusses the limitations of attempts to interpret historical
processes psychoanalytically. Nevertheless, once one is ac-
quainted with psychoanalytic method, it is difficult to resist
the temptation to apply it to collective historical phenomena.

Concepts from the domain of the psychology of the individual are often used in collective contexts. The notions of
repression or projection, for example, are readily applied
to collective cultural phenomena. However, when we get
down to the details of psychoanalytic events and their complex dynamics in the collective historical realm, we feel we
are treading on very thin ground. Jung's teachings about
mythic archetypes lend themselves more to such manipu-
lations and perhaps are the best key for a discussion of
this sort. I will now present an additional hypothesis to
explain the phenomenon of the *Golah,* this time resorting

* Saul Friedlander, *Histoire et Psychoanalyse* (Paris: Éditions du
Seuil, 1975).

to several psychoanalytic principles that in a certain sense integrate a number of the elements referred to in the previous hypotheses. Anyone who is put off by psychological terminology applied to the collective domain can regard the psychoanalytic terms and language I use here as being nothing more than metaphor.

To elucidate the *Golah* conflict of the Jewish people, two basic concepts must first be clarified. In the collective consciousness the concept "God" is equal to the concept "father" and the homologous concepts "earth-land-motherland" are parallel to the concept "mother." This, I think, is widely accepted. The identification of God with father is a feature of the consciousness of many nations and many religions; and in the consciousness of the Jewish people as well, God clearly represents the father. The concepts "earth," "land," and "homeland" are feminine, as in "Mother Earth" and "motherland."

The phenomenon of the *Golah* is, in my view, a disturbance of the proper and harmonious balance in the consciousness of the people between the father and the mother, between God and homeland.

When we speak of the singularity of Judaism we refer in the main to its monotheism, that is, to a conception of the unity of the godhead. That, and not necessarily the nonmateriality of the godhead, is the Jewish innovation. The Greek philosophers and the developers of Eastern religions also conceived of God as having a spiritual essence. But the unity and singularity of God are the special Jewish contribution to the history of religion and culture.

How was this monotheistic consciousness attained? How did a people become the bearers of the monotheistic message in the ancient world? By the image it had that it was God who gave birth to the people, or, put differently, that the father alone and exclusively, and not the mother, gave

birth to the people. This image was built up by means of a
series of myths strongly internalized by the people.

Wasn't God able to find an "Abraham" among the inhabitants of Canaan? Of course he was. But he had to assert
his supremacy over the feminine element, the homeland, by
picking out an individual from outside Eretz Israel, uprooting him from his natural and true homeland ("Go forth
from your country, from the land of your birth, and from
your father's house"). He asserts his supremacy over the
homeland in that he, the father, bestows the new homeland. The homeland is not natural, not a matter of course
("For unto you have I given the land . . ."). To stress the
existence and singularity of the father, the primal tie with
the natural mother must be overturned and destroyed and
an altogether different kind of bond be established.

The same story recurs at the nation's inception. The nation is born in the *Golah,* not in its homeland. Its natural
homeland (Egypt) is not its true homeland. That will be
given it by the father after an exclusive covenant is sealed
with him. How great is the symbolism that the covenant is
made in an intermediate region between the *Golah* and the
true homeland, in a place that is no place, that cannot be
identified physically and be linked as a place, as a land, to
the covenant. And all that to establish the father's absolute
supremacy over the mother. What is more, the nation is
commanded by grave and cruel commandment to wipe out
all the inhabitants of Eretz Israel, the Land of Canaan, in
order to destroy any possibility of a natural homeland attachment to this land. An attachment without the mediation of the father appears inherently sinful and defiling.
Many interpreters have struggled with the problem of the
command given by God, giver of the Torah, the righteous
ethical God, to destroy the peoples of Canaan utterly. The
repeated emphasis in the Bible on the need to destroy all

these peoples, beyond the requirements of ordinary conquest, stems from the latent desire to impair fundamentally
any possibility of natural relations with Eretz Israel without divine-spiritual mediation.

A people needs a homeland. Otherwise it cannot be a
nation and will remain a religious sect spreading the message of monotheism with no success. Since there is no one
in the world without a mother, the Jewish people, too,
must have a mother, but this mother is held fast in the father's grasp and he keeps constant watch over her relations
with the son. The mother-land-earth is given to the people
by the God-father, and he lays down the rules of the giving
and stipulates its conditions. The nation's contact with its
homeland is not a simple natural contact, matter-of-course
and unconditioned, like that between a person and his
mother. The mother given to the child by the father is no
simple mother; she is a mother with divine essence. She is
presented first of all as wife of the father, and the son must
be exceedingly careful with her honor, her sanctity, and
most of all, lest he defile her. The expression "to defile the
land" and the warning against doing so are repeated obses-
sively in the Bible. When the relationship between the son
and the mother deepens, the jealous father immediately in-
tervenes and claims not only that "they abandoned him"
but that they are "desecrating" the mother. Any deep and
direct relationship with the mother is immediately denounced by God. Nothing was more abominable in the sight
of the prophets than the cult of the earth. All the agricul-
tural rites had to undergo transformation, screening, and
sublimation by the godhead system. The word *homeland* itself is very little used in Jewish terminology. It is one of Judaism's more neglected concepts.

The natural balance between father-God and mother-
homeland has been disturbed in the consciousness of Juda-

ism by the dominance of the father. The sanctity of the land and its apotheosis only intensified fear of it. It was transformed from mother to woman (the father's wife), and therefore any reckless contact, without the father's supervision and permission, becomes incestuous and invites the severest punishment.

In the *Golah,* relations with the father-God are easier (the mother is distant; only longing is directed toward her). God must compensate the son—deprived of his mother because of his sins—with greater intimacy, and the son must remain close to the father, for he alone will restore the mother-homeland. And since God makes sure that a natural homeland relationship is not established with another land, which would be a new betrayal of Him, the *Golah* existence succeeds in reasonably stabilizing this entire ambivalent system. As long as she is remote the mother can maintain her important position, and the father preserves his exclusivity without losing the people, for it retains the homeland in its consciousness. The son's existence frees him of the hazards of having to tread gingerly between the father and the mother. Any possibility of attaining a new mother is immediately suppressed by the father, who preserves the son's spiritual bond with the mother by carefully interweaving the mother-homeland into every conception of final redemption.

Small wonder, then, that the *Golah* served this distorted system well as a neurotic solution. As early as Second Temple days the Jews discovered the special virtues of this form of existence. Nor is it at all surprising that Christianity, which regarded itself as a religion reforming Judaism, had to begin its reforms at the most problematic point: the exclusive power of the father. Dividing the father into three was the first step, the beginning of relief, after which the mother-homeland was released from his grasp and the female divine holiness fused with the Holy

Mother. The Christians could thus pursue a moderate monotheism, in a form that did not drive them to flight. The Jews, by contrast, maneuvered themselves into a situation whose terrible hazards became apparent in the course of time.

AN INTERIM SUMMING UP

I have offered several hypotheses to explain the depths of the Jewish people's attraction to the *Golah*. I am sure that these speculations will arouse opposition among readers for being too "abstract." Can it truly be said that a Jew from some specific country did not come to Eretz Israel in some specific period for these abstract reasons? Were issues of "chosenness" or the potential conflict between religion and nationhood actually in his consciousness? I am prepared to venture an affirmative reply. Of course, on the surface there were practical reasons and ready excuses for his not coming, but underlying these were deeper reasons related to the spiritual fetter of the Jewish self-image shared by all those who remained in history as Jews. Let us not forget that the Jewish people in any period is always a remnant, and as is the way of remnants, it carries along with it deeply embedded deposits for good or bad. But even if these speculations are rejected, the answer to the riddle of the *Golah* must be sought in the territory where I have been groping. For it is impossible to describe Jewish history as unparalleled faithfulness by a people to religious and spiritual principles and at the same time to claim that the course of this history was chiefly determined by a clinging to the "fleshpots." If we take the historical situations of the Jews throughout their history and remove the outer shells of time and place, we arrive at a number of transtemporal common factors, myths and underlying concepts that motivate us all. We play out our roles according to several fixed patterns. The decor is constantly being changed, the actors are replaced, the style differs, but the text basically repeats itself. It is that way for many peoples, it is that way for us, and a core chapter in this text is the *Golah*.

If we truly want to grapple with the *Golah* substance within us, we have to change several basic Jewish concepts. The fate of the "Third Commonwealth" will be like that of its predecessors unless we get to the root of the matter. In the early days of Zionism some long-range intellectual experiments and reexaminations of a number of fundamental concepts began to be made. Those who understood realized that it was both dangerous and futile to go on as before. The atavistic forces within the nation are too great and powerful for Zionism to ignore them. However, the physical struggle to establish and maintain the state exhausted all the spiritual energies that were being focused on a thorough elucidation of basic questions; what is more, the Holocaust gave birth to the illusion that the great debate with the forces of the *Golah* had been decided by history, cruelly and once and for all.

Most astonishing of all is that the Holocaust, stemming as it did from the *Golah* existence, did not eradicate the *Golah* virus. The nation reverted to its way with amazing swiftness. Zionism imagined that history had now provided the final conclusive proof of the terrible danger looming in the *Golah*, but the overwhelming majority of the people thought otherwise. It transformed the Holocaust into another episode on the long road of suffering traced out by inexplicable Jewish destiny.

The *Golah* has been regaining strength as of late, not numerically, but in the weight it has in the balance between it and Israel. The *Golah* which aids Israel is at the same time a threat to Israel. The steadily growing group of Israeli Jews, who base their national identity solely on the State of Israel, must hold out against the *Golah* and the forces of the *Golah,* which may yet undermine the sovereign existence achieved with so much toil and effort.

Exile, an abnormal state, proved itself effective as a possible mode of Jewish existence. It causes suffering but averts a more serious explosion. Like any neurotic solution, it is unable to bring happiness and should not be thought of as a permanent solution. But it at least prevents the crisis which, it is thought, cannot be handled. Better a manageable and familiar neurosis, with which a modus vivendi can be maintained, than an unknown reality in which the nation must stand exposed before a jealous and demanding God, proving to itself and the world by its total concrete actuality that it is the chosen people, that it is a kingdom of priests and a holy people.

However, in the present century it suddenly became apparent that this neurotic solution is the source of too great a burden of suffering, which impairs our ability to cope with reality. The Holocaust revealed the depths of the abyss along the edge of which the Jews made their way and intended to continue to make their way until the end of time. This grave conflict with the non-Jewish surroundings appeared more menacing than the internal conflicts that the nation had tried to avert, or at least postpone.

Zionism is a process of self-liberation from the fears of "independence." Its method is to point out the worse alternative. At its most profound and at its best, Zionism was the beginning of a process of self-awareness, a shattering of the vicious circle in which the nation had been entrapped from its inception: Exile, chosenness, religion-nationhood. Zionism's vitality stemmed from the nation's distress; its impressive successes were made possible by the assistance it received from objective reality—"the misfortunes of the

Jews." In an obscure way the Gentile nations, for their own reasons, helped Zionism. They understood how "abnormal" Jewish existence is and feared the murderous conflict toward which it was dragging them. The decisive step was taken. The all-embracing total Jewish reality was created; independence was renewed. But a mere thirty years after the state was established, disturbing signs of the *Golah*'s recovery already began to appear. The world's most resilient people has already learned the laws of the new modern reality and is adapting its exilic being to it. The existence of a center allows it to strike deeper roots in the *Golah*, for it now has "insurance." Concern for Israel and involvement in and for its political and social affairs accord it legitimation. And in Israel the *Golah* is becoming a real alternative to life here. It is becoming a constant presence enticing to many young people in time of real or imagined crisis. What must we do to keep the Third Commonwealth from collapse? What can we do to ensure the confidence of the 20 percent of the Jewish people enjoying national independence in the continuity of their existence here and in the long-range future of the Return to Zion?

CHANGE OR ADJUSTMENT OF UNDERLYING NOTIONS

There are peoples who, having suffered terrible national defeat, did not continue to pursue their previous course but tried instead to learn from their failure. They subjected themselves to serious self-scrutiny and by gradual and continuous effort tried to change or adjust some of the fundamental values of their culture and national character in order not to fail again. A gradual effort of this sort can be observed among an ancient and consolidated people such as the Japanese; it is trying, with sophistication, to exchange its militaristic and authoritarian values for democratic values and economic productivity. After two thousand years of such problematic history, neither can we continue as usual. To assume that the Jewish people, which has been shaped by a very special set of values, can simply be "poured" into the precast mold of a modern state is nothing but naïve. It is necessary to alter some of the people's most fundamental notions, and above all the conception of chosenness or difference. We must see ourselves as an integral part of humankind, neither superior nor inferior, different only within the normal range of difference obtaining among all nations, races, religions, and tribes. We must adopt this position as a basic value, unequivocally, without clever and sophisticated interpretations. Whether we are better than other peoples is for them, not us, to decide. All kinds of unrealistic talk on the order of "Israel's existence can be justified only if it is a model society," or "We must not be a country like all other countries" (as if any country in the world is like all other countries), do no more than establish criteria we are unable to meet; they lead only to frustration and self-blame. The uniqueness of the State of Israel is that it is a Jewish state with specific national content, in the same way that Albania is unique. Israel cannot be the United States of America, just as Paraguay cannot be the United States of America. Israel has a full right to exist—a basic moral right—even if it has organized crime, corruption, and social injustice. We want to improve the substance and quality of our life just as any other people does, not because we have to prove our moral superiority to anyone or to justify our existence to anyone, but simply because we want to live better. The need to find difference must be gotten rid of once and for all. This difference is a fact. Its quality will be determined by the reality we shape.

We have no special message for the Gentiles and have

no a priori mission. In retrospect, something we have succeeded at may be worth copying by others.† A special people, a model society—these are empty phrases, for they depend on someone else's perception and are not within the purview of our own genuine introspection.

I repeat this simple truth, that the Jewish people is a people like all peoples, and am astonished to discover to what extent it does not appear simple to many. That is the first seed of trouble. I am amazed to see that the simple meaning of normality, the basic equality of the Jewish people with all other peoples, is not readily comprehensible to many Israelis. One cannot constantly insist on legal-political equality for the Jewish people while not acknowledging our equal spiritual status with humanity as a whole. The Bible, the Prayer Book, large chunks of our tradition and culture are overrun with this element of "chosenness." No humanistic teaching can disguise or obscure it with clever argument. We must grab hold of this deep-lying notion and slowly try to root it out. We are not the first people to try to rid itself of deep-lying notions.

THE RELIGIOUS ISSUE

Secular Zionism senses that the religious issue is a high-power explosive mine set somewhere in its path and has always preferred to neutralize this time bomb with agreements and arrangements. Memory of the bitter religious struggle against Zionism has not been lost, and those religious circles which were prepared to participate in the

† It is curious that the endeavors in which we in Israel excel and are original are precisely those which are most clearly expressions of a normal society: the army and agriculture.

Zionist movement were granted special concessions to offset their vulnerability. The religious issue is the only issue for which a status quo arrangement has been established. Such an arrangement has not been reached for social, political, or economic issues. *Status quo* is a term charged with the tension of war. There is a mighty covert war that must be kept at bay from erupting by agreement, for the emotions on both sides are intense and the slightest breach of bounds is liable to unleash a deluge. Whether it was felt (erroneously, as the years proved) that the days of religion are numbered, that by means of agreements and the legitimation granted it by the secular establishment its sting would be removed and, with its vitality institutionalized, it would die a silent death—or whether it was deemed preferable to erect a tight network of agreements as a barrier against the possibility of an uncontrollable religious awakening liable to sweep away the entire system —in either case the purpose of the status quo was in one way or another to suspend the struggle between the two codes of religion and nationhood. In a certain sense the status quo is a substitute for *Golah* existence, for it, too, serves to check and mute the conflict ever present in the total Jewish life system. The difficult security situation always served as an effective reason to preserve the status quo and to avert unnecessary conflicts over this issue. But the dim, persistent feeling was that when peace came, it would be over this issue that the "war of the Jews" would break out. Until now the most violent clashes between citizens and the government, and among the citizens themselves, always had a religious backdrop, or a religious backdrop disguised as national. Most of the governments have fallen over religious issues. The covert religious-national conflict burns fiercely, and the escaping sparks are an indication of how hot and scorching is its flame.

Some religious Jews have opposed the idea of status quo. They argue that it neutralizes in advance the struggle over the character and identity of the state, for, relying on this arrangement, religious Jews have fled from the necessity of waging their war. We secular Jews regard it as a wall standing between us and the religious, but in their view the status quo not only prevents secularist domination, it also forms a natural obstacle which can justify the fact that they are not waging total war over all aspects of life.

This is not the place to enter into the complex tangle of questions raised by the religion-nationality conflict. Suffice it to say that this conflict is one of the roots of that neurotic solution called the *Golah*. This conflict is perpetual, profound, and of the essence, but it must be brought into the open; at some point it must be brought to a head. The pain of decision is at times preferable to the terrible fear of the conflict itself.

If there is genuine desire to extirpate the *Golah* option— at least for the Jews living here in Israel—a slow and steady effort must be made to change the definition of the Jew, to strengthen the national element at the expense of the power of the religious component. The distant but clear goal, the aim of these efforts, is to establish the definition of a Jew such that a Jew is a person who regards the State of Israel as his state or country: in other words, so to strengthen the national component in the definition that religion or other spiritual content cannot fill the vacuum existing in the generally accepted minimal definition (the Jew as child of a Jewish mother, or someone who identifies as a Jew). A long-range goal this, which perhaps will be attained in another hundred years. A change of definition of this sort is dramatic and revolutionary. To accomplish it, the power of the religion must be weakened, some of its fundamental values undermined, and most important, new sources of authority created within it.

What we need today are religious reformers, possibly from the periphery of Orthodoxy. They would receive powerful support from the Reform and other movements, which themselves must undergo a process of rapid and thoroughgoing Israelization. To put it bluntly, religion is too important to be left to the religious. Secular Jews, or those so called, must make their way into religious matters, not as *baalei tshuvah*, romantic penitents, but as courageous reformers.

When the secularists were in power they offered the reforming movements next to no assistance. The extent to which they cold-shouldered them is astounding. There are several reasons for this: (1) This issue was especially sensitive for the religious. They were prepared to make concessions on many issues, provided their exclusive religious authority was left unimpaired. (2) The American tone of the reforming movements seemed inauthentic and artificial to Israel's leaders, who had been nurtured on East European conceptions of Jewish authenticity.

Had Ben-Gurion, at the height of his power and spiritual-intellectual influence, gone on Yom Kippur to pray in an Israeli-style Reform synagogue, instead of secluding himself in his house to read Spinoza and Aristotle, his vast authority would have stamped a different religious conception with decisive legitimation. It, in turn, would have undergone a profound Israelization and would have become a new source of authority.

There can be no hope for a genuine normalization of the Jewish people without thoroughgoing treatment of the issues raised by religion. If we want to see meaningful change in another hundred years we must begin planning for it now. What is required is a searching and rigorous secular interest in religion, for no factor or element within the Jewish people is more powerful. To wage a total frontal war on it would be meaningless, since the human need for religion has profound psychological roots and has its own laws of ebb and flow (as can be seen today in the Moslem and Christian worlds; there is always escape to religion when reality becomes complicated and incomprehensible). The only reform the secularists want is an easing of the burden imposed by religion, but that is basically misguided. The problem at the first stage is not to lighten the burden of the commandments but to expose them to the complexities of life, to observe them while changing them. The Jewish religion ˙endures amazingly unchanged even under Jewish sovereignty in Eretz Israel, for Jewish Orthodoxy is unable and has no desire to change. Change will come about only by creating additional centers of authority, by fragmenting the religious community into sects, thereby revealing the clear superiority of the national component common to all.

WHAT CAN BE DONE NOW

Several practical conclusions can be drawn and some concrete steps taken right now. Were the Prime Minister of Israel to appear at the opening of an Israel Bonds drive in the United States and, instead of speaking once again of Israel, the territories, the PLO, and relations with the United States, speak only about *aliyah* and make a gala announcement that this year the State of Israel refuses to accept money from the *Golah* in angry response to the fact that only money "immigrates" to Israel, but not Jews; were Israel's leaders dramatically to denounce the lack of immigration and declare that all the funds collected in the *Golah* in the coming years will be allotted to one purpose only, to *aliyah;* were the State of Israel to stop sending teachers, educators, and emissaries to Jewish communities that do not meet a minimum *aliyah* quota—perhaps these dramatic acts would make an impression and would help place the issue of the *Golah* and the grave consequences of the absence of *aliyah* at the forefront of Jewish consciousness. I have no illusions that millions or even hundreds of thousands of Jews would come to Israel in the wake of actions of this sort, but even an additional few thousand *olim* would be almost a revolution in this field.

Today, for example, about 2,000 Jews immigrate to Israel annually from the United States. Ten or twenty thousand would be revolutionary in every respect, especially in terms of Zionist feeling. Although 20,000 is no more than about half a percent of the Jewish population in the United States, an immigration of this magnitude would put an end to the creeping demoralization in the country and would tie another 100,000 Jews to Israel by bonds of kinship and friendship. Can this be achieved? It may be possible. At the least the first steps in that direction can be taken. The struggle must be for the small numbers—instead of a lot of noncommittal talk to the millions, addressing a few forcefully and clearly. The souls of the few potential candidates for *aliyah* must be fought for, they must thrust into a conflict with their non-Jewish surroundings, they must be invested in. Zionism has always been built by the few. Had 50,000 fewer Jews arrived with the waves of immigration in the twenties than actually did come, there would be no State of Israel today. There would be nothing. Ten thou-

sand Jews in the days of the Second Aliyah did the work of
millions. The small numbers are the most significant. There
is no belittling them.

In recent years Israel has become a very familiar presence in the *Golah* countries, especially in the United States.
Paradoxically, it is no longer necessary to go to Israel in
order to be in it. It is now possible to receive bits of Israeli
reality in the *Golah* itself. The sense of remoteness and
mystery that once enveloped Israel has disappeared. The
modern communications media have contributed to this,
but not solely. The deepening close relations between the
Golah and Israel have blurred the boundary between them.
Perhaps it was believed that in this way hearts would be
made ready for *aliyah*, but reality has proved the contrary.
A legitimate reality of *aliyah* substitutes, of pseudo-*aliyah*,
was created. A certain sense of alienation between the
Golah and Israel, a kind of controlled estrangement, must
be reestablished at whatever cost.

A sizable group of Jews has created a framework for the
most intimate relations with Israel's leadership. They have
more knowledge of classified matters in Israel than parallel
groups in Israel itself. At a price of about 3 percent of Israel's state budget the *Golah* has purchased full legitimation for itself. World Jewry has become an acknowledged mediator in our relations with governments. This
mediation, which we avoided—in my view, most correctly
—in the early years of statehood, introduces an unhealthy
element into the normal relations between states: internal
pressures manipulated and exerted on issues of foreign policy.

The mutual dependence between Israel and the *Golah*
has greatly increased. The *Golah* is spiritually dependent
on Israel. Our political conflicts, economic problems, and
to some extent Israeli culture are the spiritual nurture of

Jewish identity in the *Golah*, substitutes for Talmud, Kabbalah, and responsa. Hence there is little reason to fear that the *Golah* would sever its ties with Israel once we initiated an ideological conflict about *aliyah*. Spiritually the *Golah* is no longer able to stand on its own. It will never be able to give up Eretz Israel as a component of its spiritual and ideological makeup. Eretz Israel is now the State of Israel, and that cannot possibly be ignored. Many Jewish intellectuals bemoan the *Golah*'s "spiritual enslavement to Israel." Cutting the *Golah* off from Israel would put these intellectuals to the test of providing real spiritual content without Israel. The *Golah* would then discover its deep spiritual dependence on Israel, its hunger for Israel. That being the case, we need not fear a severing of ties. Attempts in that direction will probably be made. But that part of the Jewish people (which we can refer to as Jewish people A)—in my estimation numbering about 1 or 2 million of the 11 million Jews in the *Golah*—which is profoundly attached to Israel and Judaism and which provides "Jewish services" to 6 million other Jews (Jewish people B)‡—that part of the people which is bound to us so intimately can no longer cut itself off from us. We now have the power—soon it will be too late—to induce in it a shock and crisis by demanding that it take a clear stand in the ceaseless spiritual contest between here and there. Since our hand is firmly grasped by it, by thrusting and letting go we can draw it to us. This is a gamble: I do not deny it. But given the fact that all the teachings, tactics, and strategies for voluntary immigration have been tried and have come up with nothing, the time has come to attempt this

‡ Jewish people C is the 3 or 4 million Jews that are already completing their assimilation, and can be considered only as French, American, Russian, and so on, of Jewish origin.

new strategy. This is a struggle for the souls of the leaders
of the Zionist federations, the members of the youth movements, the fund-raising activists, the community center
program directors, the petition signers, and those who take
part in demonstrations. This warm and loyal group must
be presented with a sharp and unequivocal demand.

Peace would liberate us from our (imagined) dependence on the *Golah* and would give us back our pride. Instead of cultivating Jewish education for its own sake in
the *Golah* we should speak of nothing but *aliyah*. Sometimes too much Jewish education dulls the needs to come
to Israel. Instead of trying to entice and persuade, with
imaginary inducements, we should expose the pathology of
the *Golah*, the amorality of that position which regards
both Israel and the nations of the world as a guesthouse, a
travelers' inn. Now that Israel exists, there is no more ex-
cuse for that existential schizophrenia which gave birth to
the formula of Exile. Those who want bits of Israeli reality
will have to find them only here in Israel. An end to the
stream of emissaries, lecturers, dancers, and singers who
flood Jewish communities in order to give them a pseudo-
Israel there. No more talk about problems and values, but
the problems themselves and the true test of the values in a
total reality.

Our stand toward the *yordim,* the emigrants from Israel,
derives from this. Our denunciation of them and refusal to
grant them work in Jewish institutions will have moral validity, because we denounce and reject the *Golah* experience as a whole. As long as the *Golah* itself is not wholly
denounced, our disapproval of only the *yordim* is tainted
with hypocrisy.

Do we heed yet another internal dispute? Will it help?
My answer is yes. The conflict with the *Golah* will first of

all expose what is special about us who live here vis-à-vis those who live outside of Israel. It will once again reveal what the major things are, those things for which we are fighting here: freedom, independence, the realization of Judaism in a total reality. Instead of fighting tooth and nail over issues of one dunam more or one dunam less, we would do better to discover that the real dispute concerns other issues. The substance of our life differs from that of the *Golah* and the differences should not be obscured. While spiritual life in the *Golah* resembles the life of a man who built his house on the waterline and is always preoccupied with one and the same question—will the water surge into his house and what kind of unrelenting efforts must he make to keep it out?—we, on the other hand, resemble the man who moved his house and set it a distance from the waterline. The question of the need to be different, assimilation, intermarriage, Jewish education, the erecting of barriers before the Gentile, participation in the life of the Gentile state and reservations about doing so—these issues are no longer relevant. We can direct all our energies to building and improving our house, to genuine creativity.

I believe that the desire to return to Eretz Israel, to live an all-embracing Jewish life, is latent in every Jew. I will never forget the wonderful story from the days of illegal immigration from Morocco in the late fifties. Boats would secretly collect Jews from Morocco, which was already under full Moroccan rule. One day a boat arrived that was supposed to take on Jews from a remote village. For whatever reason the Jews did not arrive and the boat could stay only to first light. The *aliyah* agents went to the nearest Jewish community, knocked on the doors, and said: "Are you ready to go to Israel right now, immediately, without any further thought? Take what you can, pack a bag. Don't let

the opportunity slip by." And indeed, quite a few answered
the sudden call and left everything without further ado.
This, too, is an element latent in all of us.

I am always amazed to discover anew in conversations
with Jews abroad, intellectuals, businessmen, and profes-
sionals who are well established in their affairs and places,
that they do not rule out the possibility that one day they
will come to live in Israel. Ninety-nine percent of them will
never come to Israel, but still they do not rule out the possibility of their coming. That needs explaining. It is not
mere talk lacking all sincerity. Every Jew living in the
Golah has a "redemption gland." The path of the person
who wants to come live in Israel is strewn with a thousand
and one personal and spiritual obstacles, but it is a decisive
fact that there is a small minority that did this of its own
free will. That minority proves that it is possible.

For thousands of years Jews have said "Next year in
Jerusalem," and at one and the same time meant and did
not mean what they said. It is the same today. But in the
last generation a new type of Jew has been created, the
post-exilic Jew. This Jew carries the memory of ancient independence, of the fact of the *Golah* that has failed, and of
the experience of independence restored. His entire Jewish
identity was forged in an all-encompassing reality, and on
it he has staked his entire identity. This type of Jew can
never again leave for the *Golah*. For him the *Golah* is an
option that is no more. The "heavenly Jerusalem" will
never again be a substitute for earthly Jerusalem. By its
very existence this group of Israelis—I don't know its size,
but it is growing—carries the most powerful antibodies to
the historical phenomenon of *Golah,* and unmincingly,
without hypocrisy and with integrity, it must lead the great
debate between Israel and the *Golah*.

BETWEEN RIGHT AND RIGHT: ONE RIGHT AND ANOTHER'S

The old one hurries along. The drivers are switching on their engines. That is all he needs, to be left overnight in this arboreal silence. Before he goes he would just like to know the watchman's opinion of the dumb Arab. The lorry driver has got the idea into his head that the fellow is laying in a stock of kerosene. . . .

The watchman is stirred. "Kerosene?"

"Daresay it's some fancy of that malicious driver. This Arab is a placid kind of fellow, isn't he?"

"Wonderfully placid," agrees the fire watcher eagerly. Then he walks a few steps around the old man and whispers confidentially: "Isn't he a local?"

"A local?"

"Because our forest is growing over, well, over a ruined village. . . ."

> *"A village?"*
>
> *"A small village."*
>
> *"A small village? Ah—"* (*Something is coming back to him anyway.*) *"Yes, there used to be some sort of a farmstead here. But that is a thing of the past."*
>
> *Of the past, yes, certainly. What else . . . ?*
>
> A. B. Yehoshua, *Facing the Forests*

The question of the historic right of the Jewish people to Eretz Israel, one of the first issues to occupy the Zionist movement, is—we discover to our surprise—still with us.* Once again it insinuates itself into the debates we hold among ourselves and the arguments we present to the world. For years we thought that it had ceased to be relevant. It appears now that it was only dormant. After the Six-Day War, the issue resurfaced in all its acuity: was sometimes more intense, sometimes less. Today, with the peace process in full swing and the necessary stage of a temporary-permanent settlement with the Palestinians no longer to be avoided, the question of the historic right of the Jewish people to the Land of Israel once again emerges as a key issue, this time in debates about the future of the West Bank.

Even those who believe that the Jewish people has a his-

---

* It turns out that debates about the Jewish people's right to Eretz Israel have been pursuing us since earliest times—both in the Bible, in the story of Jephthah the Gileadite (Judges 11), and in the Second Temple period.

toric, religious, or other right to the entire territory of western Israel must distinguish between right and obligation. A needy person is entitled to receive welfare, but he is not obliged to accept it and can forgo it for whatever reason if he so chooses. A person having the right to vote does not have to vote. Put differently, every person and every nation has the right to waive a right. In the political context a person can claim, for example, that the Jewish people has the full historic right to annex all of the territories of Eretz Israel captured in the 1967 war; however, since he is worried about a binational state, or about torpedoing the peace with Egypt, or about American economic pressure, he is ready to waive that right. Even the most extreme hawks among us have indicated their acceptance of this principle. All those who believe in historic right agree that it encompasses not only western but also eastern Eretz Israel, and some extend the promised borders even farther. The symbol of the Irgun shows a map with the Land of Israel clearly on both sides of the Jordan. But I believe that today almost everyone would be prepared to sign a peace treaty recognizing the Jordan River as the final eastern border of the State of Israel. In other words, the overwhelming majority are ready to renounce claim to an area of nearly 90,000 km².† Thus, when it comes to demands for expanded borders, the greatest extremists would cede 77 percent of historic Israel and the moderates 88 percent. The difference between them is 11 percent. I don't deny that that 11 percent is very significant and that we can have some very serious debates about it. I merely want to stress

† That, of course, depends on the historical period chosen for determining the borders. Jordan's territory is a little over 90,000 km², and western Eretz Israel is about 27,000 km², but eastern Eretz Israel, as understood in the period of the First Temple, and especially during the Second Temple, was considerably smaller than Jordan, about 40,000 km².

that all acknowledge the right to relinquish the right: the
question is, how much to relinquish. Thus the question of
one's obligation to historic right is not the focus of the political debate.

On the other hand, a position which claims that we have
no historic or other right to the West Bank may still recognize that the vital interests of the State of Israel require
that we keep those territories for security reasons.

Despite the frequent reference in political debate to the
concept of right, I would like to suspend its validity as a
decisive argument and neutralize its political immediacy,
so as to be able to discuss it in an atmosphere of calm de-
tachment. I would like to convince those who argue that
for security or political reasons we must hold on to Judea
and Samaria to stay with me, to follow my argument without fearing that by doing so they are abandoning their own
political position.

At this stage I would like to reveal the conclusions to
which I hope to lead the reader.

1. I will argue and try to prove that the concept of historic right has no objective moral validity when applied to
the return of the Jewish people to its land.

2. I will also try to prove that the Jewish people has a
full moral right to seize *part* of Eretz Israel or of *any other
land*, even by force, on the basis of a right which I shall
call the survival right of the endangered.

A GENUINE QUESTION?

Some people maintain that the whole issue of historic right
is artificial. Does the Englishman question his right to live
in England? Does the Indian ask whether he has the right

to live in India? Why, then, do the Jews get themselves into such a tangle? Human history is replete with conquests and annexations and nobody bothers about them. What nation has had to provide a historical accounting for its actions?

But, it seems, it would be difficult to charge that our self-laceration over this difficult issue was initiated by us. We did not raise the question; it was the Arab world, and in its wake the world as a whole. Had we found Eretz Israel devoid of inhabitants, the question of whether the Jews have the right to settle there and establish a state would not have occurred to anyone. Had we begun to return to Zion one hundred years earlier and established a Jewish state in the middle of the last century, had we come here *en masse* and wiped out or exiled the local inhabitants as many others have done in the countries they have conquered, the argument about our right to the country would never have been raised. There would not have been anyone to raise it. A "socially conscious" film director might make a moving film about the cruelty of the Jews, just as Americans have recently been making films about the extermination of the Indians in their country. But the debate about historic rights would end at the movie theater exit. It would not reach the United Nations, governments would not deal with it, and countless books and articles would not be written about it.

We are confronted with the question of right as a pressing moral issue because the country was not empty and because the residents were not eliminated or exiled; moreover, they have powerful relatives who add weight to their arguments. Thus we are called upon to answer the question of right first and foremost by an insistent outside plaintiff; the question is not only an internal Jewish question.

There were those among us who wanted to absolve themselves from having to deal with the question, claiming that in the relation between nations the question of rights is irrelevant. The world is a jungle and we behaved accordingly. Force is the *only* language between nations. This claim, which under certain circumstances can indeed be employed, cannot be used by us, since the justness of our cause was made part and parcel of our interest. Indeed, it is an important component of our political strength. Were we really strong, perhaps we could allow ourselves to use the language of the jungle. But for us it is dangerous, because its use would, for example, justify Hitler. He also claimed that all of human history is nothing but a war between wolves, and that the difference between him and the others was that at least he wasn't hypocritical about it. In other words, those who make this claim have no right to accuse either the Nazis or any other of our persecutors throughout our long history. Some who advance this argument might be willing to relinquish this right of historical accusation if by doing so they were freed from having to deal with the question of right. But that is becoming existentially more and more difficult. Even great powers like the United States, the Soviet Union, and China often resort to moral justifications. Moral issues prevented the United States from employing all its force in Vietnam. China might have driven much deeper into Vietnam, perhaps even with the backing of the Western world, but the moral obstacles to doing so became a very real political obstacle. Relations between states today (as opposed to moral relations within states) have become increasingly exposed to the rules of moral behavior. The balance of forces in the world today having become so complex, there is now a clear interest in infusing political arguments with issues of morality.

We simply cannot have recourse to the law of the jungle as a way to absolve ourselves from having to deal with the question of right. Whoever tries to do this merely legiti-

mates the use of force by others against us. He gives the
Soviet Union, for example, a green light to squash Israel.

At the same time, however, we had to use force in order
to exercise our right; right alone can create no reality. But
there is a basic difference between the use of force ensuing
from a right and its use without such a basis in right. A
person has the right not be robbed or murdered, but this
right by itself will not prevent him from being robbed or
murdered if he does not enlist the aid of active and passive
forms of power through the state apparatus to implement
this right. No one denies that Zionism also had to be realized by force. The question is whether the use of force was
justified. We have to come up with an answer, not so much
for ourselves as for that plaintiff who places his argument
before the world to judge.

THE CLAIMS AND COUNTERCLAIMS

The argument advanced by the Palestinian Arabs from the
earliest days of Zionism right up to the present is very simple: "The Jewish people had no right to come here, either
as a nation or as individuals. This land is our land and
homeland, and it is of no importance whether we consider
it a separate entity or part of a larger Arab territory. Here
we are exercising a natural national right of a people to its
homeland, or part of a people to its homeland. Your very
coming here without our permission is an act of aggression,
and we therefore have the right to self-defense. Even if you
build a home in the desolate Negev or drain a swamp in
the Jezreel Valley, we consider it aggression against us.
The question, therefore, is not who fired the first shot; we
did that, but we did it in self-defense."

All the arguments about the Balfour Declaration, the

League of Nations decision to establish a British mandate, and the UN General Assembly resolution to partition the country have, of course, no moral force whatever. These bodies had no moral authority; they had only political authority. The Arabs argue that Eretz Israel did not belong to the British (even according to their own testimony, and certainly in the Jews' view); the British therefore had no right to give it or a part of it to anyone else.

The same holds for the resolutions of the UN General Assembly. It is an organization without moral force. Indeed, it barely has any political force. (And we, of course, would be the last today to grant any moral authority to the General Assembly, even though it is now far more representative than it was in 1947.) Who gave the United Nations the moral right to partition the country? Were the United Nations to decide to divide Denmark between the Danish people and some other people, would that decision have any moral force?

The claim that the country was "no-man's-land," in the sense that the inhabitants were not organized in an independent political framework, is also morally groundless. More than half the world, in Africa, Asia, and parts of Europe, was not independent politically at the beginning of this century and lived under foreign domination. Lack of independence cannot be a reason, nor is it therefore permissible to add to the injustice of the Arabs' being denied their independence by expropriating their natural right to a homeland and implanting another people in their midst. Did the British when ruling India have the right to plant another people among the Indians, a people wanting partial or full sovereignty in India? Did the fact that we lacked an independent political framework here in the thirties and forties give the British the right to settle Bedouins from Saudi Arabia among us, and to grant them national rights at our expense?

Furthermore, the argument that the Jewish settlers were making the desert bloom, however true, cannot morally justify the Jewish penetration into the area. The Negev, under our control for more than thirty years, is still in the main desolate and unsettled, but has this diminished our right to it? Of course not! The same is true of the Hula swamps and the Hefer Valley, which were stinking waste-lands in the hands of the Arabs for generations. Their right to these areas did not expire because of that desolation.

Neither did the purchase of land grant a right. First of all, land bought from the Arabs constitutes only a small part of the territory of the State of Israel within the Green Line (which marked the borders between 1949 and 1967). Most of the land accorded us by the 1947 partition plan was desolate land not belonging to anyone (e.g., the Negev, large parts of the Upper Galilee). The land belongs to the people, just as the Nevada desert belongs to the American people and the Alps to the Swiss. The land beyond that granted by the 1947 partition was conquered in the War of Independence. But even the land bought and paid for in full does not compromise the nation's sovereignty over it. Land is not only a commodity, but also a basis of an identity. Even if wealthy Saudi Arabians buy up all the land and buildings in London, the British people will still retain their right to London as part of their homeland and will remain sovereign over it. It is interesting that the attempt to buy land from private Arab citizens led Zionism to the correct notion expressed in the basic conception of the Jewish National Fund, that land, even if private property is built on it, remains in the perpetual ownership of the nation; the nation leases it to the individual but does not sell it.

The argument that the Jews are entitled to take the Land of Israel from the Arabs because they are more developed culturally and are ready to invest more materially and culturally in the land than the Arabs is morally very dubious. We would first have to determine what is high culture and what is low—but who is authorized to range cultures on such a scale? The Germans, many believe, had a high level of culture and produced superb works of art and intellect. Did that give them the right to conquer and annex Poland, whose culture was deemed inferior? And if we mean by culture technical civilization, by this logic Sweden has the moral right to conquer all of Africa.

I am rapidly summarizing many elements included in the Zionist argument for our right to the country. None of these elements, viewed separately or taken together, give us the moral right to take this country, or even part of it, from another people. So we come back to the basic argument. And to it we must respond with a universally valid moral reply. No other will satisfy the plaintiff, and any other is liable to boomerang and legitimate an undercutting of our current rights to the country. The question is: By what right did the Jewish people come to this country at the beginning of the century, when the Jews were an insignificant minority within the population (in 1900 there were 50,000 Jews in Eretz Israel, and about 550,000 Arabs), and say to its inhabitants, "Your land is actually my land!"?

THE RELIGIOUS REPLY

The religious reply is based on the divine promise recorded in the Bible which designates Eretz Israel (within much wider borders) as the land of the Jewish people. Since God is the source of morality, His promise has moral force for us and for others.

But this answer has a number of fundamental limitations

and can in no way serve as a meaningful moral reply. First of all, only religious people who fully believe in everything written in the Bible and behave accordingly have the right to use the religious argument. A person cannot say that he accepts the word of God about the religious right to Eretz Israel, but not about how to "deal" with a wayward woman, *shmita* (the religious requirement to let the land lie fallow every seven years), or the ban on lending money to a Jew. Whoever accepts God's authority cannot be selective about it, since he would thereby place himself above God. Whoever claims this right for himself also allows the Arab to be selective as he wishes and to argue cynically that he is ready to accept the entire Torah except for the Promise. Since religious people would take vigorous exception to the secular use of divine promise to establish the Jews' right to the country. Religious Jews would sometimes suggest to the secularists that they use the divine promise, to link themselves to the religious system as a whole. You want God's word to serve as a moral and metaphysical support to our being here. Then with all due respect observe the other *mitzvoth* (commandments) as well.

Secondly, even a religious individual who is at one with his beliefs and accepts the divine promise as absolute must realize that while this promise has force for him it has no moral significance whatever for the party demanding a reply, just as a Moslem, Christian, or any other belief has no moral force for us.

The Arab will say, and with justice: "So you genuinely believe that God promised you this land, but in the Koran, in which I and 550 million other Moslems believe, it is expressly written: 'And you shall fight against those who do not believe in God and on the last day and if they will not forsake what God has forbidden them, if they do not observe the true religion, and those who were given the

Book [in other words the Jews] *will pay their dues in their hands and will be subservient.*' Are you ready to respect this belief of mine and to accept my behavior in accordance with it?"

The basis for moral dialogue and discussion can be found only *outside* the framework of the various religions. If a Hindu came to me and said that Vishnu had commanded him to take my house from me, I would answer him, "With all due respect for your God, and however genuine your faith—and I am ready to accept that it is genuine—you'll have to provide *me* with a convincing argument on the human-moral plane if you want me to hand over my house to you."

In a certain sense it was the Jews, dispersed among the nations, who helped induce people to speak in general human and moral terms transcending the bounds of any particular religion or faith. We were reviled in Christendom, a living witness of what happens to a people who betrays its God. But we insisted and still insist that the Christians determine their attitude toward us in accordance with moral principles, not in accordance with the principles of their religion, and that they resolve the contradiction between these two systems themselves. The religious position concerning Eretz Israel (held by individuals who are at one with their beliefs) can be very meaningful for the Jews, but it has no concrete moral significance for the Arabs.

It was interesting to witness the Jewish attempts to organize Christian and Moslem theology to acknowledge the Promise. As long as these were attempts to persuade—so be it. But we cannot be the final arbiters of how the members of other faiths must behave. Would it not be ridiculous and bizarre if PLO figures started explaining to us that if we are to be faithful to our religious beliefs we should remain in the *Golah* and await the coming of the Messiah? They could quote suitable chapter and verse about the justice God did by dispersing us among the nations, they could recite Midrashim about the ban on hastening the End, could quote from our ancient and modern sages about the Exile's value for the life of the people, about its creative and spiritual power. And thus, on the basis of our own theology, they could give apparent moral force to our expulsion from here. We would reject this out of hand! Our theology is our business, just as their theology is theirs. Discussion of moral issues that determine actions can be carried out only on a human-moral basis.

Religious Jews themselves, by the way, never regarded the divine promise with the same utter seriousness as those religious-nationalistic groups which are today trying to impose it as a religious duty. First of all, that the entire religious camp without exception is ready for political and practical reasons to renounce claim to more than 90 percent of the area encompassed by the Promise, and does not deem this a religious transgression, indicates that the promised borders are considered to be more a vision for the End of Days than a concrete commandment of the same status as all other commandments that must be observed in daily life. Second, there are differences of opinion among the rabbis about even the obligation to annex Judea and Samaria. No such differences exist about the eating of pork or the observance of the Sabbath.

The attempt by certain religious circles to place the issue of Eretz Israel at the forefront of the struggle is actually a desperate attempt on their part to halt the deep-reaching secularization of the Jewish people, a process that has been going on since the beginning of the century. The strength of this process is redoubled in Israel because here the normal national elements of territory, language, and a political framework are threatening to replace many of the religious elements which until now, especially in the *Golah*, have formed the core of Jewish identity. Aware that a reordering of Israeli society in the spirit of the Torah and Halachah (Jewish religious law) is not possible, these circles are trying to bind Israeli society to them by means of a national challenge infused with religious meaning.

To summarize, while the divine promise can serve to validate the religious Jew's sense of his right to Eretz Israel, it has no moral significance for a plaintiff who not only is not religious but also is not a Jew. The religious answer can satisfy neither plaintiff nor judge.

THE HISTORIC RIGHT

Zionism has in the main relied on the argument of historic right. *All* Zionists of all ideological and political shades have used it. It appears in A. L. Eliav's book *Land of the Heart,* as well as in the writings of Jabotinsky and the political lexicon of the Betar movement; it is also found in the lexicon of all streams of the Labor movement. The concept also appears in Israel's Declaration of Independence: "By virtue of our natural and historic right" (the concept "natural right" here refers to the right of inhabitants to their homeland).

The idea of historic right was based upon two fundamental arguments:

1. Up until 1,850 years ago the Jewish people lived in this land as a sovereign nation (relatively sovereign, like most nations during those times) and as a majority, and

lived here continuously for 1,300 years (except for the short Babylonian exile, and even then a large portion of the people remained in Eretz Israel).

2. During the long years of exile the nation never ceased to regard Eretz Israel as the Jewish people's only land, a land to which it intended to return, and with which it maintained a rich historical, spiritual, and psychological bond.

Thus Eretz Israel is the nation's original country, and its right to it is greater than that of those currently living in it, even if they are a majority.

As for the status of the non-Jewish residents of the land, three basic positions were advanced. The first position viewed the Arabs of Eretz Israel as having no rights, national or individual. Although the Jews forgot to leave a number of large eye-catching signs here and there in the country, announcing that "the Jews have left but intend to return, do not enter, leave the country alone," those who came here should have realized that this country does not and would not belong to them, and that their coming here was a mistake. Whether we want them to stay or go is our decision, which depends on their good behavior. This view was held by a tiny minority within the Zionist movement (this minority has been growing in the past few years), although even those who held it agreed that it wasn't the Arabs who expelled us from here, if in fact we were expelled. (I will return to that question later.)

The second position was that the Jewish people has a historic national right to Eretz Israel while the Arab inhabitants have individual rights as residents. That was more or less the position of the overwhelming majority of the Zionist movement, at least until the 1940s. The country be-

longs first and foremost to the Jewish people; the state to
be established in it will have Jewish symbols and forms;
and its interests will be Jewish and Zionist, according to
the Zionist definition that the State of Israel belongs not
only to its citizens but to the Jewish people as a whole. The
Arab inhabitants will have the right to equality before the
law as citizens of the state, the right to elect and be elected,
to observe and preserve their religion, and to special con-
sideration of their minority status, but they will not have
any overall national right. This view was shared by the
Revisionists, the General Zionists, and the majority of the
Labor movement.

The third position held that the Jews have a historic national right to all of Eretz Israel and the Arabs have a natural national right to all of Eretz Israel. These two rights
can be reconciled only by partition of the country between
the two nations.

All of these positions hold in common that historic right
is the moral basis for the return of the Jews to Eretz Israel
for the purpose of establishing sovereignty there. The concept of historic right became a cornerstone of the Zionist
movement's argument about the legitimacy of the return of
the Jews to this country. And today, too, it is a principal
argument in the current debate about the Jewish people's
rights of ownership in Judea, Samaria, and the Gaza Strip.

Does this concept have moral validity? I intentionally
emphasize the moral aspect because it is at the core of this
contention. We aired it before the world, not as a political
or legal concept (although we did try to buttress it in that
way as well), but primarily as a moral claim directed at the
sense of natural justice supposedly inherent in everyone.
The argument of historic right was directed to world public
opinion (including Arab public opinion) and not to an in-

ternational high court of justice, which in any event has no
authority to adjudicate in such matters—not at least, until
the world accepts international law as binding.‡

THE IMPOSSIBLE CONDITIONS OF HISTORIC RIGHT

When Zionist leaders, particularly Moshe Sharett, first
began to raise the issue of historic right before international forums, the response was: "Imagine what would
happen were nations to have recourse to this type of argument. The whole world would be overturned, nations
moved, borders changed. Were every nation to claim its
historic right to wherever its forefathers once lived thousands of years ago, the result would be total chaos. How
can we accept such an argument?" Moshe Sharett replied,
"The fact is that other nations are not advancing this argument, only we are, and therefore you needn't fear to accept
our claim to historic right."

In principle, Moshe Sharett was right. That a particular
principle is not relevant to most cases but is relevant to
only one or two exceptional cases does not mean that the
principle lacks moral validity. Sometimes the most exacting
legislative work is done in order to find a just solution for a
single exceptional case. But still, the moral test of a princi-

‡ But we must be able to distinguish between law and morality.
At times they coincide, at times not. The legal system of the
U.S.S.R. is far from moral, as is the case in many countries. The
Nazis, too, had a legal system. International law has not laid down
any binding stipulation concerning historic right. At most, there
have been some attempts to elucidate the problem. One such
attempt is the book by Professor Yehuda Blum, *Historic Titles in
International Law*, which does not deal with the present problem.

ple is whether it can hold for all possible similar cases in the past and in the future.

Thus, to examine the validity of historic right, we will formulate it as a general proposition: Every nation which has lost its homeland will continue to maintain its right to it, and this right will be greater than, or at least equal to, that of any other people which in the meanwhile has taken hold of the land and has made it its homeland.

Does this proposition appear just? At first glance—yes. An international morality can be established only on the basis of moral principles that obtain on the individual plane. A man who has a house which for whatever reason he has to leave retains his right of ownership to it. Whoever takes over the place in the meantime does not thereby gain title to it.

Should this principle be qualified by some time limit? On the individual plane such a time limit—a statute of limitations—usually does obtain. If it exists for murder, it should certainly exist for property. But when referring to the life of nations, we are talking about historical time, and in this sense it would be best not to impose a time limit on a people's ownership of its country. On the basis of moral principles we can assert that a nation, as a timeless entity, retains its right to its country eternally, or as long as it continues to exist as a nation.

Morally, however, formulation of historic right must be qualified by two conditions:

1. The nation must prove that it is the original, genuine, and exclusive owner of the country that has been taken from it; in other words, that it itself did not take it by force from another nation.

2. The nation was forced against its will to leave its homeland, did not merely abandon it, and was truly unable to return to it within a reasonable span of time.

The first condition is obvious and derives from the rules of natural justice. A man takes possession of someone's house by force, lives there for some time, and later is forced to leave; a second man then moves into the house. Does the first man have the right at some later time to demand that the house he himself had seized be returned to him? Obviously not. The first expropriator's claim is in no way superior to that of the second. In a certain sense the former's infraction is greater, since he took the house from its genuine owners, while the latter took it from someone who himself had seized it from another.

We want to act in accordance with the rules of justice. A nation was forced to leave its country two thousand years ago, and we claim that it still retains title to the country. If it returns, the nation that in the meanwhile took up residence there has to make way, or at least continue on as a tactful subtenant. This is, however, tenable only if the owners are *really* the owners. If they themselves had been conquerors, they can hardly lodge a complaint against other conquerors. Their claim to ownership is based on conquest, as is that of the new owners.

That the Jewish people conquered the land is related in full detail in the Jewish Scriptures, and its historic right is clearly rooted in conquest. The right of the Arabs also stems from conquest. Here someone will undoubtedly argue that the original conquest took place over 3,300 years ago. But what difference does that make? Having stipulated that time is irrelevant with reference to nations, and that therefore a nation can claim a historic right on the basis of residence 1,900 years ago, then that right can also be nullified on the basis of a conquest made 3,300 years ago.

That is why historic right cannot serve as a principle in the relations between nations. There isn't a nation (except perhaps for the Chinese and some other ancient peoples) that can prove authentic ownership of its land. Thus the only right that can stand is the right to a homeland: the right not to be uprooted from your homeland, even if that homeland was acquired by force.

But the second condition qualifying the moral validity of historic right places the Jewish people in an even more difficult position. When we argue that a nation retains its right to a homeland taken from it by force, and that this right is not bound by any time limit, we assume both that the nation was forcibly expelled and that it wants to return to its homeland as soon as possible. We would think it very odd were a nation to leave its homeland and settle elsewhere en bloc or dispersed in many places, and then hundreds of years later were suddenly to remember its homeland and seek to return to it and to oust those who had meanwhile settled in that abandoned country. Can a land be left void of inhabitants with any assurance that others will not make their home there? That land once again becomes a part of nature, and nature belongs to all mankind.

History has some harsh things to say about the Jewish people's attitude to Eretz Israel. The Jewish people was not ousted by force from its homeland, but left it (and continues to ignore it today). At the time of the Second Temple, half of the Jewish people lived outside of Eretz Israel of its own free will. The Roman exile—and historians will bear this out—did not uproot masses of people from here. Only a few were forcibly removed. Eretz Israel was gradually emptied of Jewish inhabitants because Jews did not stay here; they preferred other lands. Moreover, throughout their long history the Jews, as a nation or singly, made no serious effort to return to Eretz Israel even when they had the opportunity to do so. The non-Jewish inhabitants of the country are not the Romans who destroyed the Temple, but people who wandered into a desolate land in the course of the natural migrations of populations. Some of them lived here even earlier. That the Jewish people was and still is reluctant to return to its land has become decisively evident in the past hundred years. Despite waves of venomous anti-Semitism, despite the Holocaust, despite the fact that the State of Israel exists and its gates are open to every Jew, as of today only 20 percent of the Jewish people lives in Israel!

That historical bond, talked about so much by Zionist leaders as granting a right to this land, a bond truly profound, rich in content, and encompassing all levels of national consciousness, is perhaps the most telling testimony to the fact that the nation exchanged its actual return for a bond. But does a bond grant a right?

If the Palestinians maintain a deep spiritual bond with Eretz Israel (Palestine) for the next hundred years, pray for it, send emissaries to visit it, place its dust upon their heads, remember it on joyous occasions and on days of mourning, remember the name of every village and every city where their fathers and forefathers lived—will this bond grant them a right greater than that of those who live in the country?

The abstract principle of historic right could perhaps grant a nation that was forced to leave its homeland the right to return to it and to exercise sovereignty over another nation that had meanwhile taken its place, but only if the two further conditions had been maintained:

1. The returning nation is the original owner of the land and did not take it by conquest.

2. This nation was forcibly ousted and tried to return to its land immediately thereafter, so as not to create an ownerless situation that would enable another people to take up residence there.

These two conditions were not met by the Jewish people and, it might be added, have not been met by any other people in a similar historical situation. Hence the argument of historic right as presented by the Jewish people does not withstand the test of natural justice. And so we are back where we began and must again ask: Is the Zionist enterprise altogether devoid of moral validity?

THE RIGHT TO SURVIVAL

Since the very beginnings of Zionism the entire Arab world has confronted us with the following question: "By what right do you come here to take our land, or part of it?" Even those Arabs who today recognize our existence (and there are quite a few) and are willing to live with us in peace recognize *the fact* but not *the right* of our being here. In my view the peace process is incomplete as long as it is based only on a recognition of fact, not on an acknowledgment of justice.

I have tried to explain that all the political answers are not relevant because the question is asked not at the political but at the moral level. The Soviet Union, for example, could have presented Czechoslovakia with a political explanation for its 1968 invasion; it might even have gotten a resolution passed in some international forum approving the invasion, or have proved that the invasion fully complied with the rules and regulations of the Warsaw Pact and as such was perfectly legal. But under no circumstances could it come up with a *moral* justification.

I have examined the principal responses to the Arabs' question one by one and have tried to prove that they do not stand up to the moral test, do not meet the criteria of mutuality and universality. The moment we raise the arguments to the plane of absolute principle they lose their moral validity.

I imagine that what I have said up to now has angered many. On the one hand, what I have said clashes with their deep (and correct!) feeling that the Zionist enterprise is just, even if not in all its demands and actions. But on the other hand, they find it difficult to formulate a suitable moral reply.

Our emotional evolvement in this issue is so deep that we easily lose our objectivity in discussions of this sort. Nevertheless, had I told the story of Zionism and the conflict with the Arabs in the guise of another story about distant and strange peoples, or had I translated the Arab-Israeli conflict into a set of relations between two individuals, and asked for an objective judgment based on a sense of justice, I am almost certain that all the claims about historic right, religious right, the Balfour Declaration, making the desert bloom, and so forth, would be rejected as insufficient.

I would now like to argue for what in my view is the only valid right. This argument was always part of Zionist argumentation, but somehow was muffled and not given the force it deserves. I will call it *the survival right of the endangered*.

I will begin, as usual, with an instance on the individual plane. Assume that we are judges and that a homeless man is brought before us. He wanders the streets, has no place of his own. Living this way endangers his life and the lives of the members of his family, and he is likely to die soon as a result. Would we condemn him if he invades *part* of someone else's apartment, holds it by force, and makes it his own home, a refuge for himself and his family? Despite the complaints of the man whose apartment was invaded, we would probably exonerate him, because his act was necessary and he had no other choice. The injustice is preferable to that man's death. But all this on condition that the invader take over only part of the apartment. Were he to take over the whole apartment and throw out the previous tenant, leaving him to roam the streets homeless, we would be unable to approve his actions.

The man whose apartment was invaded would undoubtedly cry, "Why in my house? I am aware of his desperate straits, but let him move into the neighbor's house." This argument, with all the genuine hurt it contains, is obviously unacceptable, since the neighbor would raise the same protest.

On the interpersonal level and within an organized collective framework, a solution for a homeless refugee can be found, for example, by having the collective build him a new home. The situation is immeasurably more complicated on the international level.

In the modern age, especially since the national revolutions of 1848, national consciousness began to take such shape that an independent sovereign framework became one of the conditions of survival for every nation. As more and more nations attained sovereignty and established their independence, the need to achieve independence became more pressing for those nations which were not yet sovereign. As long as there were multinational empires united under a monarchy or the Church, nations were able to manage without an independent political framework. But when the state became a powerful uninational framework, all nations were forced to opt for self-determination as an existential matter of the utmost importance. At the end of the nineteenth and the beginning of the twentieth century, many nations lived in *their homelands,* but without having yet achieved self-determination. The issue of their independence became most crucial. But several nations found themselves in a situation even more grave. Like the others they, too, lacked sovereignty, but neither did they have a homeland. I shall not attempt a historical explanation of why peoples such as the Armenians, the Gypsies, and the Jews wandered the world for centuries without a homeland in which they comprised a majority, although such a comparative explanation would undoubtedly help us to understand this phenomenon. These peoples themselves certainly bear a share of the responsibility for this situation (the historic responsibility of the Jewish people for its dangerous exilic situation has been becoming ever more apparent in the last thirty years), but in terms of the needs of existence that is a fact of little importance—a people without a homeland finds itself in a most dangerous situation in the modern national world. Lacking sovereignty, it is deprived of the means to try to defend itself and assume responsibility for its fate; dispersed as it is among other nations, the *points of friction* with them become more numerous; and because it is not concentrated in any specific territory, it does not have even the territorial strength of a minority that lives among a majority. A nation without a homeland is not a minority, it is an alien group, and the difference between those two categories, as far as existential security is concerned, is significant.

Proof of how dangerous this situation was provided in our century by the Holocaust that rained down on the Jews and the Gypsies in World War II. It is perfectly apparent that if the Jewish people had had a parcel of land over which it was sovereign, the Holocaust would never have assumed the enormity it did. In the course of its history the Jewish people has had a number of temporary refuges, some better, some highly questionable, made available to it by the kind mercy of various nations, but its basic situation was always hazardous. Before World War II the Jews were accorded a relatively good refuge in the United States, but still this haven was unable to save the Jews of Europe during the Holocaust as an independent Jewish state could have done. The Americans simply did not want to open their gates to the refugees. True, no state accords absolute security, only relative security. In principle, Britain could come under massive attack tomorrow and be conquered just as Poland, France, Belgium, and the Netherlands were conquered. But all of these countries have the possibility of defending themselves. They all have political independence, which provides them with the possibility of countering any such challenge.

People sometimes argue against this right to survival by pointing out that in World War II Eretz Israel was almost overrun by Rommel, and that even had there been an independent Jewish state here, it would have been destroyed by the Nazis. I don't know what the Nazis would have done with an independent Jewish state, whether they would have acted any differently than they had in Belgium or Holland. It is not altogether unfounded to imagine that they might have concentrated the Jews from occupied Europe in such a state: prior to the Final Solution there was the Madagascar

Plan for the concentration of all Jews. Hitler first of all wanted to "cleanse" Europe of its Jews. Only later did it become apparent that nobody wanted to receive these Jews, and that to carry out this "cleansing" he had to destroy them. But whatever the truth of the matter, the inhabitants of an independent Jewish state would have died on the battlefield and not in the gas chambers (and there is a basic difference between these two ways of dying). The right of survival, which obtained throughout Jewish history but was raised to a new, more intense level by the establishment of secular national states throughout the world, has given the Jewish people (as well as the few other peoples who have no homeland) the *moral* right to seize, even by force, part of any other country in order to establish a sovereign state of its own. It was only natural that the Jewish people would prefer to return to the place where it was once independent, with which it has constantly maintained a historic link, and which it has always considered its home. But—and this must be emphasized—its rights extended to any place whatever. Had Eretz Israel been closed to the Jews (a definite possibility, for we got here at the very last moment; had the Zionist movement been delayed by twenty or thirty years, we would not have been allowed to enter), they would have had the moral right to take by force some other place. (This, of course, is a hypothetical situation, since the Jewish people hardly wanted, or wants, to return to Eretz Israel, and no Jew would have gone to Uganda, for example, to set up a state.)

The above can be formulated as a general proposition: *A nation without a homeland has the right to take, even by force, part of the homeland of another nation, and to establish its sovereignty there.*

This statement applies to the Armenians and the Gypsies, but does not hold, for example, for the Chinese-Vietnamese refugees. Either they are Chinese and should go to China or Taiwan, or they are Vietnamese and should return to Vietnam to struggle for their rights, just as oppressed people struggle for their rights in all totalitarian states.

Those Arabs who have recognized our existential predicament (the Arabs generally tried to deny the fact of the Holocaust, anti-Semitism, and so on) claim that they are not responsible for the Jewish situation. But no nation in and of itself is responsible for the homeless situation of the Jews. The world is responsible. But since it is impossible to build a country from pieces of land taken from different countries, the Arabs as part of the world cannot prevent anyone who is fleeing death from invading their home.

The Arabs can claim, "If that is the case, then assimilate into the nations among whom you live. Many Jews have done that. Why do we have to pay for your desire to remain Jews?"

There are two cogent replies to that argument, one of a universal moral character, the other historical-factual.

1. You cannot solve someone's problem by eliminating him. To ask someone to renounce his identity is in effect to ask him to die—not a physical death, but a spiritual death. How would we react were the Iraqis to tell the Kurds that they should cease being Kurds and should become Iraqis, that in that way the Kurdish problem would be resolved? What would the Palestinians themselves say if we used that argument against them: "You suffer today as a nation that lacks independence. Stop being Palestinians, assimilate among the Arab nations, become, say, Syrians, Iraqis, or Lebanese"? Would they accept this argument as morally valid? Of course not, and justifiably so. Similarly, they cannot claim that we should assimilate.

2. The historical reply is, I think, even more edifying. Assimilation depends not only on the desire of the assimilator, but equally on the receiving society. World War II provided horrendous proof that even Jews whose most ardent desire was to assimilate did not escape the gas chambers. Many Soviet Jews were ready to assimilate into Soviet society, but the regime did not accord them that possibility. Assimilation is not a voluntary, free act; it also depends on the other side.

But, as I have noted, the very demand that someone assimilate is fundamentally immoral. It demands that the individual and nation choose death, assuming that this is an option that can be freely chosen.

Thus the right to survival is a genuine right. It derives from an objective circumstance of having no alternative. Zionism saw the approaching conflagration. History has proved that its vision was not a mere chimera.

The next question to be asked by all sides is: How large a portion of land? In keeping with the right-to-survival argument, Greater Israel adherents can claim that Eretz Israel on both sides of the Jordan is the whole land, and we are taking only part of it—the western part. And I would have to admit that their contention sits well with the line of argument advanced here.

Others claim that western Eretz Israel is the whole, and that our right extends to part of that. Incidentally, the Palestinians themselves have yet to decide what they regard to be the whole for them. The Palestinian Charter views Eretz Israel on both sides of the Jordan as the Palestinian homeland. But this is a matter for a practical rather than a theoretical discussion, although it seems to me that justice would require that the notion of whole or part relate not only to territory but also to what *portion* of the invaded nation must make way. And the majority of the Palestinian nation lived, and is living, in western Eretz Israel.

At a certain stage (1947) the Zionist movement recognized the right of the Palestinians (no one then denied their existence) to part of western Eretz Israel, as well as their right to a state of their own. This recognition was accorded by official representatives of the Zionist movement, not as a tactic, but in earnest. How happy we would have been had the Arabs accepted the partition plan, thereby sparing the difficult War of Independence, which claimed so many victims. The Palestinians' rejection of the partition solution in 1947 and their total war against us do not abrogate their right to accept now the principle of partition of western Eretz Israel according to the 1949–67 borders, just as the Jewish people's refusal during centuries of exile to return to Eretz Israel did not abrogate its right to return to it in this century. There are those who claim that when a nation is defeated in war it loses its right to its country. This is, of course, absurd. Even the Germans, who launched a war of annihilation in Europe, murdered millions, and wrought terror, destruction, and havoc, did not lose their right to Germany. And even the Jewish people, which suffered the most at their hands, did not demand that the German entity be dissolved and that Germany be parceled out among the nations. A nation is a timeless entity; it can be punished but cannot be nullified. This obviously holds for the Palestinians, whose war can in no way be compared to that of the Nazis. (Any attempt to make such a comparison only *lessens* the enormity of the Nazi horrors.)

To summarize, the right of survival gave us the moral right to come here with the intention of taking part of Eretz Israel for ourselves. The Zionist movement on the whole tried to minimize the pains suffered by the local in-

habitants as a result of the invasion. It settled in desolate
areas, did not uproot villages, tried to develop the land for
all inhabitants, used arms only in self-defense. Until the
War of Independence, there was not a single Palestinian
refugee in all of Eretz Israel. On the contrary, the arrival
of the Zionists stimulated migration into the area. But
these acts in and of themselves did not create a moral right.
The only basis for that was the fact that those in flight from
existing and potential flames had no other choice. These
fires were envisaged not only for Europe, where they actually did break out ("If you don't eliminate the *Golah,* the
Golah will eliminate you," wrote Jabotinsky in the 1920s;
some of the marvelous poems of Uri Zvi Greenberg, written in the 1920s, also intuitively foresee the approaching
Holocaust), they also could have burst out in the Arab
countries. The State of Israel rescued the Jews of Arab
countries from the grave situation, unrelated to the Arab-
Israel dispute, of an alien minority within oppressive dicta-
torial military regimes (like the situation of the minorities
in Iran today). But, as I have said, the basis for this right is
the seizure of a *part.* If we intend to extricate ourselves
from the situation of a people without a homeland by turning another people into a nation without a homeland, our
right to survival will turn to dust in our hands. We will
then be left with no language except the language of force,
and we should not be surprised if those stronger than us
will also speak in that language, including those who have
not yet done so.

I have no intention here of getting into the complex issue
of defining who are the Arab inhabitants of this land.
Today they are Palestinians, and they were potentially
Palestinians at the turn of the century, just as Syrians, or
Iraqis, or others who lived as Arabs in the Ottoman Em-
pire were potential Syrians and Iraqis during the same pe-

riod. The attempt to define them only as Arabs would make them the only Arabs in the world today. Any other Arab is first and foremost a Syrian, Iraqi, Egyptian, Saudi, or whatever, and only afterward an Arab. All such semantic exercises are futile. The entire world (including our most devoted friends) has recognized the Palestinians as a nation. Any group of people has the right to define itself as it will, and that definition does not depend on anyone else's recognition, just as how we define ourselves is no one else's affair. The Jewish people, having been dispersed throughout its history, has proposed a definition for nationhood that is correct. Consciousness is the decisive factor determining nationality. Jews living thousands of miles from each other, speaking different languages, living in different political frameworks, and even estranged from specific religious and cultural contents, have the right to consider themselves as belonging to the Jewish people on the basis of consciousness alone. How dare we say that our consciousness is determinant, but the consciousness of the Palestinians is not when, in addition, they can point to other national factors: a common territory, language, and a brief but intense history. This argument, it seems, is coming to an end. And the Palestinians, who in their charter are still trying to claim that the Jews constitute only a religion but not a nation, will also recognize that this road leads nowhere. The faster these pointless debates come to an end, the more blood and tears will be spared. But here we are already entering the political argument. The moral discussion we have attempted here will serve as a helpful background in the search for practical solutions. Morality is not the only solution to all problems, but it is a decisive element in any solution that would last.

JEW, ISRAELI, ZIONIST: HONING THE CONCEPTS

> *That is the problem. In order for our character
> to change as much as possible, we must have our
> own environs. And in order to create those en-
> virons ourselves—our character must undergo
> thorough change.*
>
> Y. H. Brenner

In recent years most of the nation has lived its life with little concern for ideological clarification. Small groups of
"hawks" and "doves," religious and secular, radical leftists
and rightists did argue heatedly among themselves over
ideological issues and engage in sophisticated clarification

and elucidation that sometimes plumbed the depths of Jewish history. But most of the nation took no part in these debates. In a certain sense, belief in and support of leadership figures, such as Golda Meir and Moshe Dayan, substituted for ideology. The question was not the ideology of the leaders but the extent to which they exuded authority, were decisive, and exhibited pragmatic thinking. The power and mystique of several key figures in Israel in recent years lay in the fact that they avoided making clear statements and were largely nonideological. The crisis of leadership following the Yom Kippur War suddenly bared the ideological vacuum that the personalities of these charismatic leaders had previously concealed. The nation tried to fasten on to other figures, but to no avail. Now and then the hope arises that here, finally, is a leader who will save us the trouble of having to think, one on whom we can assuredly rely, but these hopes do not materialize. The rate at which leadership in Israel and in the Western world is abraded is truly astounding.

It seems to me that the time has come to examine whether perhaps the pronouncement issued in Israel and in the West at the end of the fifties about the end of ideology was not a bit premature. It would, of course, be pointless to return to the simplistic and brutal ideological polarization of the immediate post–World War II years, nor is there any reason to long for the chaos of the ideological fantasies that prevailed in parts of the West in the mid-sixties. What the Western world, Israel included, now needs is a cautious return to an ideological system that will more realistically integrate the various components of modern society. The problems that have emerged in recent years in the West and in the East (of which the energy crisis is only an external manifestation) demonstrate the ultimate helplessness of the pragmatic-bureaucratic state, the form of state that has typified the West in the last twenty years. The problems of the modern era will not be solved by improving the efficiency of the state apparatus, by centralization or decentralization, by more efficient and inclusive tax collection, or by empty slogans about solving the problems of social inequalities. The decisions and solutions must reach deeper. The solution of the problems stemming from social inequality, if indeed a solution is really desired, involves a price much greater than many imagine, for it is inextricably linked to society's class structure. The issue of Greater Israel, for example, is clearly ideological; the vision of all of Eretz Israel cannot possibly be presented as a pragmatic vision that will bring peace. This vision has a price, although it is of course significant that some people are prepared to pay it. Similarly, those who advocate withdrawal from the territories on the basis of an ideological principle that opposes domination of another people cannot present their vision as the best pragmatic solution to the problem of security. The implementation of the principle of nondomination of another people involves a price in terms of security, and the price should be presented along with the principle. It will be necessary to come to a decision on the issue of religion and state, separation or nonseparation, and to be aware of the heavy price tag carried by any resolution of this issue. And a new ideological decision has to be made concerning our attitude toward the *Golah:* to continue to grant it legitimacy or to cross swords in renewed debate, taking into account the chances the latter course holds for greater *aliyah* as well as the dangers it entails of alienating large parts of the Jewish people from Israel.

A pragmatic bureaucratic state claims to provide solutions to problems by means of its efficient bureaucratic apparatus. These usually take the form of compromise, hushing up, bribery, and payoffs. While the pragmatic bureaucratic state promises the most effective handling of problems that arise, a society with an ideological center courageously chooses from among various possibilities, with the people paying the price out of a sense of having freely chosen—not a mechanism of balances and compromises, not handling problems according to the pressure they exert or their urgency, but following a course that has a goal.

Ideology in and of itself obviously cannot encompass all aspects of life in all their complexity. There are no ideological formulas that can be applied mechanically to the full steam and rush of life. Nevertheless, fundamental ideological positions (and not only with reference to the "big" issues) are significant, and persistent preoccupation with them continuously feeds the system of practical decision.

As a first step toward ideological clarification we must, I believe, redefine several basic concepts, and above all those which denote our identity. I refer to three interlaced concepts: Jew, Israeli, Zionist. They have to be precisely defined, and the set of relations between them must be finely tuned.

PRO DEFINITION

Some are drawn to the business of definition; others are repelled by it. I am definitely of the first sort. From time to time it is fitting to devote time to a precise, logical, almost formalistic discussion of the definitions of basic concepts. Words, like coins, undergo two processes: they get worn and they get sullied. There are words that get worn down and have to be returned to the mint in order to regain their precision, to have the fine engraving that constitutes their meaning restored. There are other words that have been muddied, covered over with accretions of mire, and if we are to rediscover their original meaning they have to be cleaned. The word *Israeli,* for example, is one that I think has been effaced; to regain its full delineation and significance, it has to go back to the mint. The word *Zionist,* on the other hand, is a striking example of a word that has been covered over with dirt, all kinds of elements unrelated to it having attached themselves to it, and what it needs, therefore, is a good cleaning.

To deal with definitions is richly rewarding, because the logical and factual rigor demanded by the definition sometimes leads to the root and essence of the matter. It helps separate the essential from the unimportant and dispels the mystical fog that hovers over many things, making them more problematic than they actually are.

The reluctance to deal in definitions is of two sorts. There are those who maintain that definitions are not subject to logical considerations or a survey of facts, but are instead subject to the authority of some institution supposedly responsible for providing the definition. Thus the World Zionist Organization is responsible for establishing the definition of a Zionist. Institutions can, of course, provide definitions more or less useful, more or less correct, but their authority is not incontestable. The definition must be tested by the criteria of logic and reality. The Knesset more than once changed the definition of "Jew" as it appears in the Law of Return, but the Jew's reality did not change accordingly. Were the World Zionist Organization to define a "Zionist" as a person who insists on Jewish sovereignty over all of Eretz Israel, that decision would not accord with historical fact, for there have been Zionists who did not fit this stipulation. The definition must comply with the reality of the definiendum in all past situations and all possible future situations. It must also comply with the internal logic of the concept. Hence no one can absolve himself from dealing with definitions on the assumption that this matter has been handed over to some official body. We must constantly reexamine the definitions of concepts so essential to our identity. We may be assisted by the definitions produced by institutions or scholars, but final decision and approval rests with us.

Some resist dealing in definitions for the very opposite reason. They feel that definition institutionalizes and ossifies a concept having broad subjective meaning, robs it of its freedom. What point is there in defining the concept "Jew" or "Zionist" when everyone has his own interpretation and personal feeling about it? But this course, too, is riddled with dangers. Would we agree, for example, were people to define the concept "democracy" in accord with their personal taste and inclination? Would we permit a tyrant to assert that he, too, is a democrat, by his definition? Isn't the Soviet usage of the term "popular democracy" a perversion of the concept "democracy"? Of course, we can never prevent others from employing definitions arbitrarily and improperly, nor is it difficult to discover opposing definitions of the very same term. But that does not mean that the concept does not have one exclusive definition. Several scientific theories may be proposed to explain a certain phenomenon, perhaps even contradictory theories, but in the final analysis there is *one* theory that best describes the phenomenon. Similarly, even though I cannot prevent others from presenting other and opposed definitions, I can still claim absolute status for mine and can put it to the test of public, logical, realistic, and open discussion. Especially in these days, when ideological and political polemics are becoming especially rough-and-tumble, the proper use of several basic concepts should be preserved and agreement about them maintained.

THE DEFINITION OF THE JEW: THE DIMENSION OF FREEDOM

Political debates about the definition of who is a Jew erupt among us from time to time, and one might have expected that some researcher would have already tried to discover the laws of these debates' recurrence. Ever since the Law of Return stipulated that a Jew is a Jew by his own declaration, the religious camp has mounted a relentless and consistent effort to restore the definition to its Halachic formulation: A Jew is the child of a Jewish mother or someone who has converted to Judaism in accordance with the Halachah. This attempt has been crowned with almost total success; the last phrase, "in accordance with the Halachah," still does not appear in the definition in the Law of Return, but it is almost certain that the religious camp will find the suitable coalition moment to impose this phrase on the definition. That does not mean, however, that this definition, which served our people for hundreds of years, is the ultimate in precise definition. The truth is that another definition can be offered, as follows: A Jew is a person who identifies himself as a Jew.

We discover an astonishing fact in the classic Halachic definition. According to the Halachah a Jew is not identified as such by any element having content whatsoever. Nothing is said in the definition about the Jew's conduct, his thoughts, or basic principles of behavior. There is nothing indicating his homeland or language, or even the nature of his affiliation to a specific collective (such as maintaining solidarity with the Jewish people). The definition is totally bare. A Jew is nothing more than a child of a Jewish mother, not even of a Jewish father. A person whose forefathers for generations were Jews but whose mother alone is not a Jew is himself not a Jew by this definition. Is this biological fact really so compelling and binding? Not at all! Despite its biological component, the Halachic definition is not a racial definition. I do not know how often the simple fact has to be stressed and restressed that the Jews are not a race and never viewed themselves as such. They viewed themselves only as a people. According to the Halachic definition, a Jew, the son of a Jewish mother, who converts to Christianity ceases to be a Jew. The idea that a Jew who converts remains a Jew is a widespread misconception. According to the Halachah an apostate remains a Jew only with regard to certain matters of marriage, divorce, and some others (meant to prevent conversion from being exploited as a way to be rid of obligations and thereby causing complications for other Jews); at the same time, however, the Halachah deprives the apostate of his social-national membership in Kelal Yisrael and no longer considers him a Jew equal to other Jews. That the Halachah enables someone not born of a Jewish mother to become a Jew also indicates that the Jews do not constitute a race. The concept of race refers to a closed entity, that is, to certain physical characteristics defining a certain group which can be neither shed nor acquired by effort, such as the racial characteristics of the blacks, or of the white race, or the yellow. Precisely because these features are genetically acquired and are not within the range of choice are totally without meaning. Racial membership itself is thus totally meaningless, or at least should be. If people did not attack another race as such, as, for example, they have attacked the black race, the members of the race under attack would not accord the feature that distinguishes it such untoward significance.

To be a Jew means to belong to a national group that can be left or joined, just as any other national group is left or joined. Countless Jews have abandoned the Jewish people, and the struggle now and in all generations against assimilation indicates that it *is possible* to leave the Jewish people, that the individual is not compelled to retain his membership in it. The distortion in our self-concepts and self-perception can be traced primarily to the impact of the Hitlerian conception. Whoever argues that it is impossible to leave the Jewish people, and calls upon the Holocaust for proof, is actually asserting that Hitler is the definer of the Jewish people, and that of course is absurd. Those Jews who did not regard themselves as Jews (for Halachic or other reasons) and were nevertheless herded into the concentration camps were not Jews, even though they were regarded as such by Nazi judgment. I respect their desire and not Hitler's. By contrast, those Jews whose fathers, but not mothers, were Jews, but who nevertheless identified as Jews and were killed by the Nazis as Jews, definitely were Jews even though—and how terrible a thought it is—had they survived, the religious system would have refused to identify them as such. Paradoxically, it can be said that the religious system accepts them as Jews only because they are dead and it does not have to worry about burying them (for if it had to bury them, they would have to be buried outside the cemetery wall).

We are now approaching the root of the matter. If we delve deep into the logic of the religious definition we see at its base another definition: A Jew is someone who identifies as a Jew.

Someone born of a Jewish mother is no longer considered a Jew if, for example, he converts to Christianity or to Islam. And if we ask further: What if he converts to Buddhism?—the answer is identical. And if he becomes a Hare Krishna? The same. And so on. In other words, it is of no importance where the Jew goes. What matters is his desire to leave. It must be understood that in the past, when everyone had a religious identification, Judaism ruled that passing to any other religion turns the Jew into a non-Jew. But today, when the individual is not obliged to maintain a religious identity, a person can leave the Jewish people without having to pass through a religious corridor, even if according to the Halachah it seems that he must. The determining factor is not the technical step of formal religious conversion but his desire no longer to identify with the Jewish people. A Jewish atheist can become a non-Jewish atheist; the passage through another religion is a dispensable formality.

The same holds for joining the Jewish people. The determining factor is the act of identification, free will, and not the formal conversion, which may be altogether meaningless for the convert who, let us assume, is a confirmed atheist. Even though he may present a façade of accepting the yoke of the commandments, inwardly he can oppose them altogether, and as soon as he gets his certificate of conversion he can have absolutely nothing to do with religion, just like many Jews from birth. The absurdity is very apparent here: whereas a Jew born of a Jewish mother who denies even the existence of God will always be identified as a Jew, a Gentile who wants to identify as a Jew must pass through the corridor of religion. These religious corridors (for entry and exit) may be good as a salve for the conscience of religious establishments, but they are irrele-

vant and meaningless for someone who wants to enter or
leave, and does so as a freely chosen act.

The definition I am proposing, that a Jew is someone
who identifies as a Jew, is not one I would want to be
maintained always. In the essay "The *Golah:* The Neurotic
Solution" I noted that to strengthen the national element it
is necessary to set out on the arduous task of changing this
definition, but this definition has been the realistic, correct,
and genuine definition until now. It is the base definition
underlying the Halachic definition. The Halachic definition, born in the recesses of Jewish history, was suited to a
world and situation in which religion was the decisive element of a person's identity. The secular identity taking
shape before our eyes in the world and in Israel (which always existed as a potential) exposes the deep and true
definition at the foundation of the Halachic definition, that
which declares that a Jew is someone who identifies as a
Jew.

All those who see something anarchic, or perhaps poetic,
about this definition should recall that this was the definition stipulated in the Law of Return for the first ten years
of the State of Israel's existence, and no one (except for
the religious) saw anything anarchic about it. This definition—a Jew by self-declaration—is virtually the same as
the definition of a Jew by self-identification. This definition
served unassisted as the criterion in the Law of Return at a
time when hundreds of thousands of Jews arrived in Israel
as *olim,* and it "worked" without any special problems.

All the pseudo-Sartrean theories that would base Jewish
self-identification on the existence of the Gentile (in the
best circumstances) or the anti-Semite (in the worst circumstances), who forces the Jew to identify as such, are ridiculous. I don't need the Gentile's perception or the anti-

Semite's hostility to establish my Jewish identity. Even if
there weren't an anti-Semite in the world I would still want
to identify as a Jew. How demeaning to present Jewish
identity and belonging as a kind of trap from which there
is no escape. Those endearing stories in the evening newspapers about Jews who wanted to assimilate and in the end
returned (they or their sons) to the Jewish fold particularly savored by those who conceive of Jewishness as a
fate, a kind of leprosy, and who take pleasure in finding
out that they are not the only ones "caught in the trap"!
That is obviously not so. Hundreds of thousands of Jews
have left the Jewish people for good, as a matter of their
own choosing, and have been lost forever among other
peoples. To be a Jew is a matter of choice. This element of
freedom in the act of Jewish identification has of late been
obscured, but it is an element of tremendous importance,
for it brings with it responsibility. If I identify as a matter
of free choice I assume certain responsibilities. When
young people repeatedly ask, as they have been doing with
increasing frequency since the Yom Kippur War: Is it possible to cut one's ties with the Jewish people? Is it possible
to carry out a "disengagement of forces" with the Jewish
people? Or, in the words of a soldier, is it possible to be
just a person?—to all of these questions my answer is
clear: It most definitely is possible. But if a person decides
to identify as a Jew he assumes responsibility for his
identification, since his decision was freely made. I do not
ignore the social, cultural, and family influences on a decision about identification, but these are not sufficient to determine the identification. It requires willed choice. The dimension of freedom, which always formed part of Jewish
identification and which has recently been obscured by notions of Jewish "fate" and by the experience of the Holocaust, needs to be highlighted once again. The sense of

freedom immediately lightens the sense of responsibility. A man is capable of mighty actions if he has a sense of freedom, while feeling coerced only depresses and incenses him.

✗ The element of freedom in the act of identification is also what makes possible change and reinterpretation of Judaism. I do not dismiss those who think only of continuity, who want to keep alive the "ember" they imagine has been passed on to them. But no less legitimate is the desire of those who want to introduce change in Judaism, with which they identify as an act of free will.

DEFINING THE ZIONIST: THE CORE AND THE ACCRETIONS

"Zionist" and "Zionism" are very confused concepts. Here someone speaks in the name of "authentic" Zionism, there in the name of "humanistic" Zionism, another speaks in the name of "great" Zionism, and yet another in the name of "original" Zionism. One hurls a charge of "anti-Zionism," while another speaks of "fascist" Zionism. The time has come, it seems, to lay down precisely and clearly a realistic formal definition of this term. Definitions on the order of "the link between the people of Israel, the Torah of Israel, and the Land of Israel" will not help us understand why, for example, we consider the Neturei Karta* anti-Zionists even though they would wholeheartedly subscribe to the above formula, nor why Zionists who do not at all believe in the Torah of Israel and certainly do not follow its commandments are considered Zionists. Trivial definitions such

* An extremist religious group living in Jerusalem.

as "the belief in the Jewish people's existence in Eretz Israel" or "the struggle for the State of Israel's existence" do not provide any inkling of why Zionism was condemned in the United Nations by a country such as Sweden. A Swede is permitted to love his people and country and a Jew is forbidden to love his country?! A definition such as "the right of the Jewish people to all of Eretz Israel" would place someone like Ben-Gurion outside the bounds of Zionism, for he was prepared to relinquish those parts of Eretz Israel taken in the Six-Day War. The definition advanced by the Zionist Left—"the national liberation movement of the Jewish people"—is altogether muddied. I do not know from whom the Jewish people is to be liberated. From the Americans? The British? And what about in Israel itself? Are we not liberated? Others maintain that a Zionist is someone who comes to settle in Eretz Israel. If so, what about all those who were born here: are they not Zionists? Confusion arises from each of these definitions. Often it is the result of confounding a description of historical fact with an implicit stand on a preferred behavior toward reality.

I will here try to propose formal and precise definitions of this concept. Up until the establishment of the State of Israel a Zionist was defined as "a person† who wants to establish a Jewish state in Eretz Israel."

The key word in this definition is *state*. The forefathers of the present-day Neturei Karta came to the country at the beginning of the nineteenth century and were among the most faithful settlers in Eretz Israel, but they were not Zionists because they did not want (and even opposed) the

† Some may insist on saying "a Jew," although I would certainly permit a non-Jew to identify as a Zionist. Winston Churchill called himself a Zionist.

establishment of a Jewish state here. In the above definition the word *state* is perhaps even more important than
the words *Eretz Israel*. It is not surprising, then, that when
it seemed that the gates of Eretz Israel would be shut to the
Jews, several of Zionism's most outstanding leaders began
to consider the possibility of establishing a Jewish state
elsewhere. But that, of course, was a futile fantasy. The
Jews hardly wanted to come to Eretz Israel. It was almost
certain that none would go to Uganda or some other place
to set up a Jewish state. But what is historically important
is the special emphasis on the notion of a state, that is, on
total sovereign Jewish existence as the cornerstone of Zionism. That, in fact, was already said at the First Zionist
Congress by Herzl: "At Basel I founded the Jewish state."

I know that historians can prove to me that many
Zionists both here and abroad did not think in terms of a
Jewish state. That was indeed so, for at the end of the nineteenth and beginning of the twentieth century it was not
yet adequately realized that a state was the only viable
form of national organization. There still were many intermediate forms of organization, such as autonomy, a national home, and dominion status. Many people were still
unaware that the road of semisovereignty was an impossible course to follow, that the only choice is between full
sovereignty and nonsovereignty. Of course there were
Zionists who stressed settlement, a spiritual center, the return to the soil, and for whom statehood was not a primary
objective. But if we strip the husk from the notions,
dreams, and beliefs of all the manifold groups who rallied
together under the flag of Zionism, we discover that in the
end they all wanted to attain political and social independence, and that could only be attained by organizing
into a state. If we were to press a thinker such as Ahad

Ha'am,‡ who advocated a spiritual center and rejected all talk of a state, and were to ask him to describe his vision of a spiritual center, he would have been forced to acknowledge that a spiritual center could not be created by a Jewish community living the same minority existence as all the other Jewish communities in the *Golah;* to become a spiritual center, this community would have to be sovereign. No Zionist imagined that in Israel the Jewish people would live in a structure identical to that of its existence in the *Golah.* The few Jewish settlers in Birobidzhan (U.S.S.R.) and Argentina also thought about a return to the soil, but did not consider establishing a fully independent sovereign Jewish state, for they realized that it was inconceivable that Soviet Russia or Argentina would be willing to relinquish territory for such a state.

Underlying the Zionist outlook was the ambition to establish a state. Zionism needed full sovereignty more than any other national movement because it demanded the right of unlimited immigration and unlimited settlement, and these could be realized only under full sovereignty. Obviously there were differences over the tactics to adopt to achieve the goal. Some made no bones about it; others wanted to keep quiet until a Jewish majority was created in Eretz Israel. Some thought in terms of a binational state, others about partition, and still others about all of Eretz Israel. There were socialist, religious, bourgeois, and nationalist Zionists. Each had his own dream and ideology, but common to them all as Zionists was the final goal of the establishment of a Jewish state in Eretz Israel.

Once the state was established it could be said that Zionism was "over," for it had accomplished its mission. The

‡ Ahad Ha'am (1856–1927) was one of the leading Zionist philosophers.

mountain climber ceases to be a mountain climber once he reaches the summit. And so the definition had to be changed. The desire to establish a Jewish state in Eretz Israel could no longer define the Zionist, for the state had already been established. The post-1948 definition is therefore the following: *A Zionist is a person who accepts the principle that the State of Israel belongs not only to its citizens but also to the entire Jewish people.*

That is the definition, and what is most important in it is, in my view, the last point, that the Zionist regards the State of Israel as belonging to the Jewish people as a whole. The clearest expression of this principle was given in the Law of Return, a Zionist law that has no parallel in the laws of any other people. The Law of Return grants the right of automatic citizenship to any Jew who wants to join this country. This Zionist principle establishes the special relationship existing between Israel and the Jews elsewhere in the world and Israel's responsibility for the fate of those Jews, who are its potential citizens. And those Jews living abroad who consider themselves Zionists regard the State of Israel as their country, with all that follows from that. According to this definition it is as if the citizens of Israel relinquish part of their sovereignty for the sake of the Jews in the *Golah*. There is a difference, of course, between first-class ownership of the State of Israel, that of the citizens (including the non-Jews) who have Israeli identity cards, and the lesser form of ownership offered to the Jews who are not citizens of the country. The Zionist framework only establishes the principle, while its implementation is subject to a variety of interpretations.

That is all there is to the definition. Zionism is not a substitute for words like *patriotism* or *chalutziut* ("pioneering"). Patriotism is patriotism and *chalutziut* is *chalutziut*. The language is rich enough to enable everything to be

called by its proper name. It is obviously necessary to
define patriotism or *chalutziut* and then to check against
reality to see who meets the definition and who does not.
But these words should not be confounded with Zionism. A
stockbroker may also be a Zionist even though he may not
be much of a pioneer; and a young girl who does not serve
in the army for religious reasons, in compliance with the
law, may be a Zionist even though she may not be much of
a patriot.

Zionism is not a total ideology. If someone says he is a
Zionist, he has still said very little about himself. He still has
to clarify his position on his relationship to society, on the
problem of the territories, on questions of religion and
state, on the problem of social inequalities, and other
things. Zionism cannot substitute for an ideology such as
socialism, liberalism, or religiosity. The fact is that people
who totally disagree with one another on many issues still
consider themselves, and their opponents on these issues,
Zionists according to the above definition. The bitter debates about the future of Judea and Samaria are not related to Zionism. These are very important debates, but the
various positions taken have no bearing on the question of
the definition of Zionism. Had the Arabs accepted the UN
partition plan in 1947, and the State of Israel lived in
peace within the 1947 borders, it would still be a Zionist
state, no more or less than present-day Israel. On the other
hand, were Israel to annex Judea and Samaria but to re-
scind the Law of Return, it would be a non-Zionist state
even though it stretched over the entire territory of Eretz
Israel.

A person is certainly entitled to try to link his world
view to Zionism and to make the latter an important component of it. But he must remain aware that this linkage,
however true and desirable it seems to him, is not binding

on the concept itself. He can justify the linkage he has
made, but his reasons do not preclude the possibility of a
different linkage opposed to his. For example, someone can
explain why the idea of Greater Israel suits Zionism so
well, for it is the way to prepare territory for the entire
Jewish people. Someone else may argue, on the other hand,
that the preservation of the Jewish character of the State of
Israel is what accords with the Zionist conception. Each
has his reasons, but given the definition I have proposed,
neither of them is permitted to disallow the other's claim to
the appellation "Zionist."

A citizen of Israel can define himself as an anti-Zionist
or a non-Zionist. I do not have in mind only non-Jewish
citizens of Israel. Communists, members of Mazpen,* Neturei Karta, and the various types of "Canaanites"† also
reject Zionism, each group for its own very different reasons deriving from very different ideologies. Nevertheless,
all of these groups are non-Zionist.

Defining someone as a Zionist does not require that he
do anything in particular. A Ministry of Immigrant Absorption official or a Jewish Agency emissary abroad,
whose work is to implement the bond between Israel and
the Jewish people, is not a Zionist any more than a factory
worker or schoolteacher. By definition, to call someone a
Zionist requires only that he accept the principle stipulated
in the definition, just as to be a socialist or democrat
requires not actions but acceptance of a principle. A person can be termed a socialist even if he is not a member of
a Socialist party, and a person is called a democrat even if

---

* A radical left-wing group.—Trans.
† A small political, and primarily literary, movement that advocated the development of a new "Hebrew" nation in Israel, distinct
from and unattached to Diaspora Jewry.—Trans.

he does not "do" democracy every day. The acceptance of the principle is what defines the man. Obviously we might prefer that a person try to implement the principles he espouses and may think it fitting that he try to bring his actions into line with his thoughts, but as soon as we include actions within the definition we have to assess those actions. The domain of assessment is a most questionable one, and there is little likelihood that we would ever be able to find our way in it. Thus by this definition a Jew living in the *Golah* will be called a Zionist if he accepts the principle that the State of Israel is also his country. He is not required by the definition to come to live in Israel. If we were to make coming to live in Israel a condition for being called a Zionist, we would not find a single Zionist outside of Israel.

The descriptive term "Zionist" is thus not a badge of honor pinned to the chest of the Jew but merely an expression indicating acceptance of a position that defines the relations between Israel and the Jewish people. Ninety percent or more of the Jewish citizens of Israel are Zionists by this definition, and all the parties in the Knesset, with the exception of the New Communist List (Rakah), are Zionist parties. This, however, does not make these Jews any more moral or just or in any other way better than anyone else.

According to the definition I have proposed, an Israeli Arab can also define himself as a Zionist. This may seem preposterous but should nevertheless be calmly considered. Most of Israel's Arab citizens reject the State of Israel's Zionism and are unwilling to accept it (I am speaking about those who accept the State's existence). But a situation is certainly conceivable, and I envisage its coming about once peace is achieved, in which some of the Arabs (not many) will of their own free will acknowledge the Zionist princi-

ple. Even today there are Arabs who are members of
Zionist political parties; some are even Knesset members
representing those parties. Most of them, of course, ignore
the question of acceptance of the Zionist principle that
forms part of the parties' platforms. But should an Arab
want to accept this principle, there is absolutely no reason
to keep him from doing so. In the same way, a Jew living
in Italy can accept the special relations between Italy and
the Vatican even though this is apparently a purely Catholic matter. He can argue that as an Italian citizen he can
accept or reject any particular aspect of Italy's basic position on this. A Copt in Egypt can accept or reject Egypt's
Pan-Islamic character. The same holds for the Arabs of Israel. That part of the Arab population which will in time
accept Israel's Zionist principle as binding for it will be
able to call itself Zionist. There is no reason to create perpetual estrangement between these Arabs and the state in
which they live.

The same can be said about the concept of the "de-
Zionization" of the State of Israel. Opposition to the very
existence of the State should not be confused with rejection
of its Zionist character. Certainly anti-Semitism should not
be confounded with anti-Zionism. These are distinct concepts and should be kept as such. The strategy adopted by
Israel of calling every anti-Zionist an anti-Semite will not
diminish the number of anti-Zionists; it will only enlarge
the ranks of the anti-Semites. "De-Zionization" means
nullification of the special relationship between Israel and
the Jewish people as expressed, for example, in the Law of
Return. As mentioned, the vast majority of Israel's Jewish
citizenry opposes and will always oppose such a step, but
everyone is certainly permitted to argue against this special
character of the State.

Similarly, the concepts "State of Israel" and "Eretz Israel" should not be confused. The State of Israel is a specific political concept and is what is referred to in the definition, whereas Eretz Israel is a geographical concept and does not properly belong to the definition. The State of Israel can extend over all of Eretz Israel, or part of it, or even over areas that are not part of Eretz Israel (Sharm al-Sheikh, for example, which many wanted to include within the State of Israel's sovereignty). The State of Israel is the decisive framework for the Zionist principle.

Once the nature of the definition is thoroughly elucidated it becomes possible to discover at least what to expect of Zionism and what not to expect. I have never been able to understand what is meant by Zionism within quotation marks or Zionism without them. In response to all the cries and moans of disappointment with Zionism, that "Zionism is finished," it must be emphasized once again that Zionism sought to establish a Jewish state in Eretz Israel, a state in which every Jew could find a home. Those are the only two conditions in the pact Zionism concluded with the Jewish people. And these two conditions have been met. Zionism did not promise a model society, and if some of its leaders made such a promise in the name of Zionism they were mistaken and misleading. The implementation of Zionism does not require that a model society be formed; it might be established and it might not. That depends on one specific world view which some Zionists accepted and others did not. Zionism could not guarantee absolute security for the Jewish people, and therefore there is no accepting the argument that Zionism promised to establish a safe haven but that the most insecure place for the Jewish people today is Israel. First of all, the basic contention is incorrect. Second, we seem to have metaphysical notions about security. Did the Belgians have absolute security in 1940 when Belgium was conquered in a matter of days by

Nazi Germany? More recently, did the Vietnamese and the Cambodians have absolute security? Zionism promised only the establishment of a Jewish state. Whether a state affords a people greater security is a question that must be asked on a different plane. What is meant by security must first be stipulated, and in what context. A state certainly grants a people a certain kind of security but also exposes it to certain kinds of dangers. But that is not specifically related to Zionism.

Zionism also did not promise to establish a sublime Jewish spiritual center in the State of Israel. Such a center may be created and may not. Zionism promised one thing only, and that promise it has kept: a Jew will be a free person in his state, sovereign unto himself. Therefore all the talk about disappointment with Zionism is meaningless. It is quite possible that many people feel disappointed, but they would do better to direct their sense of disappointment to the proper address—to the labor movement, the liberals, the religious, or the Revisionists. Everyone will find his own proper address. The best will search for the source of their disappointment within themselves.

To summarize, just as there is a vast difference between the definition of a Jew and that of Judaism—the definition of a Jew is simple and concise and gets right to the point, whereas Judaism is a complex system of ideas, beliefs, ways of life, historical facts, and so on—so, too, there is a difference, although not vast, between the definition of a Zionist and the concept of Zionism. We can speak of Zionism as a historical movement, we can analyze the various tendencies that coursed through it, describe the strategies of its various leaders at different periods, explain the various interpretations its thinkers gave to revolution and continuity in Jewish life, and the like. The definition of a Zionist, however, bares the essential hard core, the neces-

sary essence shared by all. This is not only a matter of
semantics, it is also a matter of principle. Since the word
Zionist appears with such high frequency in our vocabu-
lary it must be kept clear and distinct. This term is also a
major target of attacks on us from outside. In order that
we can better defend it, it must first be clarified. It must be
demystified so as not to be able to conceal or befog matters. Many debates require that their proper and precise
frameworks be found rather than always being bound up
with the concept of Zionism, as if it contained some magic.
Foggy concepts always lead to the casting of blame, exces-
sive pathos, and, in the end, cynicism.

THE ISRAELI: THE DIMENSION OF TOTALNESS

The definition of an Israeli, like that of a Jew or Zionist,
appears to be simple: An Israeli is a person who possesses
an Israeli identity card. This definition, like that of a citizen of any other country in the world, is not encumbered
with matters of content, world view, or beliefs. Such are
not essential to the definition. But behind the technical
simplicity of using the identity card as the criterion for
identifying an Israeli is a rich and ramified set of obligations and rights that bind the Israeli to all other Israelis
and to the state organization that unites them.

The word *Israeli* is in fact the original and authentic
term for a Jew, and since the content of the word has been
so drained in recent years, it is necessary to recall its origins once again.

The Jewish people took form under the name Am
Yisrael, the people of Israel, and according to its own belief God granted the people this name. Moses called him-

self an Israelite (a member of the people of Israel), as did
the prophets and kings during the First Commonwealth period. The division of Solomon's kingdom, the separation of
the Kingdom of Judea from the Kingdom of Israel, created
the first cleavage of concepts. The word *Jew* at that time
denoted only part of the people of Israel. It was used for
the first time by Jeremiah on the eve of the destruction of
the First Temple, and was used with greater frequency
after the departure for exile in Babylonia and Egypt. We
also find the term *Jews* in Persian documents, indicating
that it was used by the Gentiles to designate the people of
Israel. Ezra tried to restore to the word *Israel* its original
luster and made a point of using it rather than *Jew* in all
his writings. His practice was followed by many during the
Second Temple period, but after the Second Temple was
destroyed *Jew* supplanted the word *Israelite*.

The word *Jew* is bound up with two things: the religious
belief of the people of Israel and Jewish existence in the
Golah. The word *Israeli(te)*, on the other hand, denotes
the Jew (religious or secular) who lives a total Jewish existence, the signs of which are a land, a language, and an
independent social framework.

Whereas *Jew* always denotes a partial existence (which
is why it is apparently possible to be a Jew of greater or
lesser intensity), an Israeli(te) lives a total Jewish existence deriving from a binding framework; just as it is impossible to be more or less French, so, too, it is impossible
to be more or less Israeli.

The word *Israeli* denotes a mode of Jewish total existence that may or may not include a religious component
(just as a religious component may or may not be present
for a Jew in the *Golah*). The Israeli's totalness ensues from
the very framework in which he lives. An English farmer
who lives in Yorkshire and who never in his life read

Shakespeare is no less or more an Englishman than an Oxford don who devotes his whole life to the Bard. "Totalness" derives primarily from living in a specified territory (the prime basis of identity), from a national language, from ways of life, and from a specific society that is called upon to answer the needs of every individual comprising it.

In the *Golah* the Jew lives a partial existence, even religiously. Geography is not part of his identity; the political, economic, and security issues of the social entity in which he lives are not his to decide. In the ghettos in certain periods the Jews were able to live a life that displayed some of the signs of totalness, but because of the narrowing of life's compass and the restrictions imposed on initiative, this was no more than a semblance. Matters most basic to life were beyond the Jews' reach. Religion itself even surrendered certain commandments and values (e.g., those related to Eretz Israel and to political existence), because there was no way to give substance to them. In the last hundred years the scope of the Jew's activity as a citizen participating in the nation state within which he lived was greatly enlarged; at the same time the scope of his Jewish activities diminished even more. The political and military system in which he participated was not Jewish, nor was the economic system or the educational system. In the best of circumstances he became an after-hours and holiday Jew, and most of all a Jew in his family and social contacts. A schizophrenic existence was created, with all his energy devoted to defense of Jewish partialness, which was always liable to be swept away by the powerful current of the life led by the nation among which he lived. In recent years the Jew stopped speaking Jewish languages and began instead to speak the language of the country in which he lived; he was educated in the universities of the nation among which he lived—and so on. It was in this way that the Jewish picture of recent times was created, one of the hallmarks of which is division between realms of life not related to Judaism and realms that seem to be "Jewish." The criteria for sorting out the realms are neither reliable nor consistent. The synagogue was clearly a Jewish place, and so was the Jewish community center, which, however, soon became the site of nonreligious activities such as sports. But a hospital run by Jews also came to be considered a place of Jewish activity. After the State of Israel was established, all activity related to Israel became Jewish activity, even if it had nothing to do with religion.

An odd situation was created. Whereas, for example, a social worker in the *Golah* who works in a Jewish community center is considered to be doing Jewish work, an Israeli social worker is not regarded as doing so. A Jewish doctor in the *Golah* who works at his profession in a Jewish hospital supported by the Jewish community is considered to be doing Jewish work, but an Israeli physician in an Israeli hospital does not do especially Jewish work. An activist in a Jewish organization in the *Golah* working for the sake of Soviet Jewry is clearly involved in a Jewish activity, whereas an official of Israel's Foreign Affairs Ministry who deals with the same issue is not considered to be involved in a Jewish activity.

In the *Golah* any contact with anything related to the lives of Jews immediately becomes Jewish activity, because it is apprehended as part of the constant struggle to keep the Jews from being swept up by the totalness of the alien reality that seeks to efface and assimilate them. In Israel, where all activity is performed among Jews and concerns Jewish matters, other criteria have been established to determine what is specifically Jewish activity. As if partialness, which is inherent in the concept "Jewish," must also have its place in the Israeli situation, activities here, too, are sorted into Jewish and non-Jewish. Thus religious activity is considered Jewish activity, as is volunteering activity related to contact with Jews in the *Golah*. To deal in historical periods dating back to about 1850 and earlier is to deal in Jewish history (as opposed to Zionist history); a certain kind of literature is considered Jewish, and lately the Holocaust has been incorporated into the "Jewish" zone. From time to time, symposia are held on questions of Jewish values and Jewish consciousness, the favorite topic being "The State of Israel as a Jewish State." In these sessions two alternatives are generally presented: that Israel will conduct itself as a Jewish state, or that it will merely be the State of Israel. Those in attendance hear the classic reproach that they are not sufficiently "Jewish," that they lack "Jewish values," that they are "rootless and decadent," and so on.

The classic mold that existed in the *Golah* is reinstated in Israel: the distinction between the reality of the stream of life and some Jewish concentrate with which these neutral waters must be mixed to give them their Jewish vitality and coloration.

Israeliness is not conceived of as the fullest, most complete, and total expression of being a Jew. That we live in the land of the Jews, speak the language of the Jewish people, live in a society that has a vast Jewish majority, are governed by Jewish institutions, maintain a Jewish educational system, have a profound bond with the Jewish people, fight for Jewish objectives, and are identified by the entire world as Jews—all that, it turns out, is not sufficient to establish Israel as a Jewish state. Something else is apparently needed.

For some of us it is religion, which garbs itself in the general name: Jewishness or Judaism. But here, too, the concepts must be kept clear. If what is meant by the "Jewish concentrate" is religion, this must be stated explicitly. The question should not then be posed as how to make Israel a Jewish state, but how to make it a religious state. The questions that must then be asked are about the religious aspects of our existence. But the concept of Jewish religion, Judaism, or Jewishness are not part even of the Halachic definition of a Jew. A clear distinction must be made, calling religion and faith by their name, emphasizing the belief in God and all that follows from this belief. Mixing religion with concepts such as "Jewish consciousness" is very misleading. An Israeli may have "Jewish consciousness," and there isn't an Israeli who does not have the fullest Jewish consciousness—without necessarily believing in the existence of God, not to speak of a specific Jewish God. These concepts are misleading when used innocently—they are sometimes used to disguise religious intentions under a mantle of some vague and general Jewishness—for two major reasons: (a) the historical memory of the Jew's reality being defined primarily by religious components, since other components were not within the range of his life (especially a country, language, and a total Jewish society), as a result of which the identification Jew-religion became absolute; (b) the fact that at present there are also non-Jewish Israelis. This new situation of non-Jews living as minorities within a total Jewish framework somewhat muddles the issue. Must an Israeli consider his Israeliness as indicating a framework of membership but not of content, simply because there are Israelis whose nationality and religion differ and whose mother tongue is not Hebrew? Most definitely not. Take Iran, for example. There are religious and national minorities in that country who are considered Iranians, and they do not muddle the Iranian consciousness of the Iranian majority. It is the same in all countries. That there are French Jews does not dilute the full and complete Frenchness of the non-Jewish Frenchmen, even though those Jews have a different national consciousness and a different religious attachment. The minority presence among us is still refracted to us through the Middle East conflict, but when this conflict is terminated our attitude toward the non-Jewish Israelis will become normal. Their Israeliness need not diminish ours, nor need it reduce it to the most elementary common denominator. They, not we who are the majority in Israel, will have to live with the schizophrenia of a double identity. We can take pains to ensure that their double identity will not be too problematic for them, and therefore neither for us. This, however, will be done not by sharing a double identity of our own but by making the shared elements (land, language, and social framework) decisive for our identity, and therefore also for theirs. If they are brought into painful conflict by their double identity they can resolve the conflict by leaving for a place where their specific national identity is shared by the majority (a Palestinian-Jordanian state) or by fully joining the Jewish (Israeli) totalness, that is by becoming part of the people of Israel, of Am Yisrael. The second course need not pass only through the religious corridor. A fear of converts was a feature of our life in the *Golah*. There we hesitated to introduce other national elements into our midst, for even though they accepted our religious faith there remained the growing fear that they would retain national components in conflict with our national existence (which was more muted in the *Golah*); what is more, they would always remain in their homeland among their fellow nationals. It is, however, much less problematic an affair when we are joined by non-Jewish Israeli residents for whom Eretz Israel is their homeland and

Hebrew their language, who serve in the Israeli Army and have the experience of living within our total social framework. Many of us are the descendants of foreign peoples who converted to Judaism during the Second Temple period, a successful conversion because at that time, too, there was a structure of Jewish totalness. Precisely because we are numerically and otherwise at a disadvantage in the world and in the region, we must begin to make joining us easier, so as to change from being a society in constant fear of assimilation to one that attracts others to assimilate in it.

The more a Jew in Israel is Israeli, the deeper reach his roots here and the less the chance that he will leave the country. The more he becomes a Jew (i.e., identifies only or primarily with the religious component, or some other partial national component), the greater the chances that he will pick up his bags and move on. When an Israeli builds his identity primarily from the components of country, homeland, language, Jewish total social reality, and the sense of being self-sovereign, all of these woven into a single fabric, it is difficult for him to leave Israel, for to leave then would be to shatter his identity. But when he identifies first and foremost as a Jew, in accord with the classic components of Jewish identity as it has existed in its partialness throughout our history, the chances that he will move on from here are greater. Partial Jewish identity is the most effective passport for roaming the face of the globe, as has been proved in twenty-five hundred years of Exile. I find it necessary to explain once again the concept "partialness" that I have been using. Was Maimonides, for example, a partial person as a Jew? Certainly not in his own subjective consciousness, but definitely so in his reality. A prisoner in jail is a partial man, in the sense that a good part of the range of human activity is out of his reach. Whatever his subjective consciousness, his reality is such that he is inca-

pacitated and incomplete. A Jew in the *Golah* undoubtedly
feels himself to be whole and complete as a Jew, but in his
reality as a Jew (in terms of the range of possibilities that
the Jews and Judaism have themselves posited) he is a limited being, incomplete and obstructed. The *Golah,* or
Exile, is a partial situation, defective and incomplete in
terms of Judaism's own conception of itself.

Thus, if we are always preoccupied with finding the
common elements in the experience of a Jew in New York
and a Jew in Israel, it is no problem to pick up one's bags
and move from here to there. The Jew need not change his
identity to leave the country. He can find "Jewish sources,"
"Jewish values," and "Jewish dreams" in abundance in
New York. Available to him are numerous models of Jewish exilic identity from which to choose to mold his own:
the identity of Maimonides, of Moses Mendelssohn, of the
leaders of the Bund, of Franz Rozenzweig, of Simon Dub-
now, an identity such as that of Abraham Joshua Heschel,
or of the Lubavitcher Rebbe, or of Rabbi Soloveichik, etc.
The leaders of education in our country wave a threatening
finger at Israeli youth and warn them of the dangers of assimilation in Israel, as they warn the Jewish youngsters in
the *Golah*. But to prevent that "assimilation" it would be
better to move to New York, where there are three million
Jews who have developed much more sophisticated means
to protect their Jewishness.

But all these warnings are absurd, the product of our
many long years of distorted history. A person can never
assimilate in his own country, he can only change. The
French in the twentieth century are worlds different from
the French of the thirteenth century, but the French have
never assimilated, they have only changed. The present-day
French are no less French than those of earlier generations;
in a certain sense they are even more French, for they now

bear within them the experience of a richer and longer
French history. As long as a nation retains its language, its
land, and the total framework of society, it changes, is
influenced, but does not assimilate.

To reiterate, to be an Israeli is to be a total Jew, and it is
this totalness that is the source of our Jewish responsibility.
The Jewish responsibility of a Jew in the *Golah* is very cir-
cumscribed. In a certain sense he stays a "clean" Jew, for
as a Jew he is not responsible for the foreign policy of the
country in which he lives, nor for the army, the prisons, social inequalities, the perversions of government, and so
forth. He has his books filled with lofty values, few of
which are put to the test in actual life. In Israel, on the
other hand, every detail of life is tested against Jewish
values, beliefs, conduct, and dreams. Whoever is concerned
about the continuity of these values must examine them
not in theory but in their application. Does the way in
which an Israeli prison is being run comply with Jewish
values?—that, for example, is a real question. When soldiers in Israel's army observe the "purity of arms," Jewish
values are reinforced; and when they commit an atrocity,
Jewish values crumble. There is no longer the distinction
between a closed spiritual world within which ideas are
discussed and a reality not at all relevant to that discussion.
Much of our spiritual heritage operated only in theory, and
what is gripping, as well as painful, about Israeli reality is
that it exposes the theory to life.

Whatever happens here becomes a link in the long chain
of Jewish history, simply because it happens. Some events
are our choosing and our doing; others pick us out and
force themselves upon us. But because of our involvement
in them they are all part of our history. The Holocaust
rained down upon us from outside; nevertheless, it becomes a Jewish experience no less profound or basic than

the revelation at Mount Sinai. The distinction between the authentic and inauthentic in Jewish life becomes irrelevant when applied to total Jewish life. I believe that it was also meaningless in the *Golah,* but there the lines of demarcation between Jew and Gentile were blurred and authenticity had to claim to provide a basis for some sort of distinction. But here everything is authentic, that which is to our liking and that of which we disapprove. If the dress of Hasidim, modeled after the costume of Polish nobles in the fourteenth century, has today become a symbol of Jewish authenticity, why is the clothing of Jews who dress in the latest Parisian and New York fashions any less authentic? True, external cultural influences can be strong and rapid or weak and slow-working. There can be a powerful surge of original creativity and there can be imitativeness. There will always be those who do battle for the past simply because it is the past, and those who thirst for signs of the future. But these are normal struggles in every society and culture. Language, land, a sovereign homogeneous society always create a solid and authentic stage for all such contests and all change.

THE HONED CONCEPTS

The greater a person's self-understanding, the greater his freedom and the wider the range of his possibilities. The same holds true for a nation. Self-understanding enlarges its freedom and expands its possibilities. Such self-understanding can be achieved by study of the past, of spiritual origins, of the basic patterns that recur in the nation's relation to the world and in its image in the world, of its historical successes and failures. As part of this process it is necessary from time to time to sharpen and clarify the fundamental concepts of identity. I have tried to do that here.

The following emerges from the definition and elucidation of the concept "Jew":

1. Jewish identification always entailed a free act.

2. The Jews are not a race but a nation. The definition once again made this perfectly clear.

3. The free act demolishes the mystical notion of "Jewish fate." There is no Jewish fate in the sense we usually employ that term, just as there is no Swedish, Palestinian, or Indian fate. Every nation has the specific facts of its reality and every people has broad features of national character which were molded in the course of its history and which from time to time give rise to recurring patterns. Our character is our fate, just as the character of every other nation is its fate. And character is always subject to change or to better adjustments to the facts of objective reality.

4. The concept "Jew" denotes a partial existence that at best bears a semblance of totalness. The concept "Jew" was suited to the condition of existence in the *Golah*.

5. The Jewish religion is not identical with Jewry or Jewishness, and it cannot be Jewry's exclusive spokesman. The Jewish religion expresses only part, albeit an important part, of Jewish being and conduct. The Jewish religion and faith must be forced to expose themselves and identify themselves for what they are; that is, they must bare the foundation of belief in God and in the system of *mitzvoth* (religious commandments) that underlie the religion.

The religious attempt to define the secular Jews as "potentially religious" or as "religious deep down" must be thwarted. That is a clever stratagem concealing an attempt to deprive the individual not only of his external but also of his inner freedom. On what is deep in a person's heart only he is permitted to declare. Whoever wants to use such a technique to claim that there really is no such thing as a secular Jew or a Jewish atheist but only different degrees of religiosity must be made to know that his argument can be turned against him. It can equally be said that there is no such thing as a religious Jew, only various degrees of secularity, that "deep down" the religious Jews do not really believe but only make a show of believing, out of fear of stating explicitly what they well know—that there is no God.

We learn the following from the definition and elucidation of the concept "Zionist":

1. Zionism is not a comprehensive ideology but a specific stand with regard to a principle, a position that is compatible with various and even contradictory ideologies. It is of utmost importance to bare the Zionist common denominator of these world views.

2. Making the concept "Zionism" clear to the world can, I believe, lead to a considerable decrease in the recent attacks on it and may even renew the historical sympathy that the world has had for the process of the Jews' normalization.

3. Anti-Semitism is not the same as anti-Zionism and there is nothing to be gained by obscuring the difference between them. Anti-Semitism is a disease arising not only from prejudice, chauvinism, and intolerance of anything foreign, but also from the essentially abnormal situation of

the Jews among the nations. The cure prescribed for this by Zionism was not only to educate the Gentile but also a basic change in the Jew's situation. Anti-Zionism is related to the Middle East conflict and to hostility toward a modern, open, and democratic state able to maintain meaningful ties with citizens outside of it, even allowing them partial participation in important decisions (It is not surprising, then, that the totalitarian states are Zionism's sworn enemies.)

4. Restricting the concept "Zionist" to its proper domain clears the way for the large ideological debates, such as that about the territories, the character of the society and polity, and questions of religion and state—each under its own precise and specific heading.

5. Zionism stipulates that between the nation in Israel and Jewry in the *Golah* there is a bond of mutual responsibility, but it does not obfuscate the difference between the total Israeli and the Jew in the *Golah*.

6. By defining the concept "Zionism" we once again bring to the surface the genuine and legitimate promises made by Zionism and clear away what are only imagined promises (e.g., "to create a model society" or to provide the Jewish people with "absolute security").

The following emerges from the definition and elucidation of the concept "Israeli":

1. The total Jewish dimension of the concept "Israeli" was uncovered by going back to the word's origins. The difference between the Israeli and the Jew, in terms of the relationship between whole and part, was highlighted. That difference also exists between a religious Israeli and a religious Jew.

2. The possibility of an Israeli assimilating in Israel was refuted.

3. The Jewish responsibility of the Israeli was made apparent. Whatever is done here puts Judaism to the test. Judaism, like any culture and civilization, is tested by deeds, not only in theory.

4. The non-Jewish Israelis will be clearer about their double identity. They will share with the Jewish Israelis the elements of land and political framework, and will be distinct from them in nationality and in part of their culture. Two other possibilities are also available to them: to join the nation of Israel fully, or to leave the country and to join a separate political framework made up of their fellow nationals (i.e., a Jordanian-Palestinian state in which they will be able to actualize their nationality fully).

IN PRAISE OF NORMALITY

The attempt I have made to realign these concepts does not, of course, do away with the conflicts, tensions, cultural struggles, and constant inputs and reequilibrations of problems of identity. All it does, I think, is establish a more correct framework for struggles of this sort, which take place among all peoples and in all countries. We, who are only at the very beginning of the process of normalization, can expect struggles of the fiercest kind in the coming years. The entire world is groping with problems of identity, and we even more so. But as long as the State of Israel remains a normal state these struggles will not shatter the state framework.

I have already noted that no word stirs up as negative a

resonance among the Jews as the word *normality*. From its very beginning, Jewish history has been saturated with opposition to this concept, and Jewish existence in the *Golah* (which was meant to fulfill, in a distorted way, the impossible task of being a nation different from all others) reinforced the negative attitude toward the notion of normality, for there it was identified with assimilation. Since the Gentiles were normal we presumed that the only way to keep the Jews from becoming Gentiles was to preserve their abnormal situation. That was the source of all kinds of romantic and mystical theories rationalizing the abnormal situation, trying to justify it and give it purpose.

On the individual level we are well aware of the difference between the normal and the abnormal (with all the problems of borderline cases). On the interpersonal plane we do not esteem abnormality, nor do we bedeck it with notions of "great spirituality," of "holiness," of "purpose," or of "originality." Rather, we see its pain and agony, its basic limitations, and in the best of instances acquit it with pity. We know full well that the normal is not something vague, banal, homogeneous, or standard.

Normality is nothing but a rich and creative pluralism in which a man is as sovereign as possible over his deeds and the range of his possibilities is great. We have no adoration for a homeless nomad, nor do we believe that he has some real advantage over a family man anchored in his work and land. We know how to distinguish between abnormality and nonconformity. We know that many works of genius of the human spirit were created in conditions that could be considered very normal, banal, and conformist. Abnormality is clearly identified as an illness, a misfortune that fundamentally distorts the individual, paralyzes him, and depresses his world.

Jewish history in the *Golah* displayed the symptoms of

abnormality, even as the Jews themselves conceived of it. We felt the pain of our situation, felt the severe limitations imposed on our possibilities, and never lost the feeling and the knowledge that we must get healthy again, that we must get out of this situation. That hope of being redeemed never abandoned us, and that was our good fortune. The central stream of Jewry lived with this feeling. Only a few tried to idealize our abnormal situation, to make an ideology of it, to justify it by a theory that "God did us good by dispersing us among the nations," or by conceptions of the "normal or religious mission of the wandering Jew," or by theories of "special creativity in the *Golah*" and such.

The Holocaust brutally and horrendously showed us the abyss into which we had fallen as a result of our abnormal situation, of our being not "like all the nations"; it revealed the terrible cost in blood of theories about "mission," "special creativity," and the like.

The establishment of an independent Jewish society in the State of Israel gives us a framework for a cure, but the cure itself can be effected only by a persistent, continuous, and aware effort. Some have tried to interpret the Arab-Israeli conflict in terms of fate in order to prove the basic, almost genetic, abnormality that accompanies us in whatever situation we find ourselves. This conception is counter to the central spirit of Zionism. This conflict is a national-territorial conflict and there have been sharp and protracted conflicts like it in human history; there are nations that have fought and are fighting for their independence and the world's recognition for hundreds of years. But even this our conflict is coming to an end. The peace with Egypt is the first step in the process, from which there is no going back. And when peace comes and the normal framework of the State of Israel finally wins recognition from the world community, and especially from the nations of the region in which we live, we will come to know that normality is not to be abhorred but, on the contrary, is the beginning of a new period of manifold possibilities in which the Jewish people will be able to shape its fate, create its culture in full, and participate in the shaping of mankind as a full partner with equal rights in the international community. It will turn out to be the best way to be different and other, singular and special (like every other nation), without constantly fearing loss of identity.

THE CONSTANT SHADOW OF WAR

Before Thursday afternoon arrived and two agitated carts made their way up to the top and Mota roared—Hey, on your feet, soldier boys!—not a man of them gave a thought to all the rumors that had been cropping up for some time already, as if something would arrive, or as if they would be moving on to someplace else, nor to all the other signs which were plentiful and detailed enough—so much did a rash action like that run against all reason and logic.

Try to imagine—to go out now to look for trouble! And who? Them again. If there was anything they had coming to them it was a handshake, some few but moving parting words, and to be sent off for two or three weeks' leave. Instead, suddenly on a clear afternoon, they come and take you and throw you who knows where—like nothing. As if you were still that green that after some fancy talk you get all whipped up, grab a Sten, and run and jump and gallop until you fall. Hardly. Shaul, in the dab of shade under the tamarisk, would go on grumbling and pro-

testing—however you figure it the sum comes up
the same—leave; look at the facts this way or
that and they still say—leave; and what about
justice—then for sure leave. As for the others—
have they run out of kids and all kinds of pusses
from the country, always, always us?

S. Yizhar, *The Days of Ziklag*

The Jewish society in Eretz Israel has been engaged in a conflict for about one hundred years. It should not be forgotten that the State of Israel's present conflict with its neighbors is but a continuation of one that began almost at the very moment the first Zionist set foot on this soil. There have been occasional lulls in this conflict—truces, cease-fires, temporary interim agreements—but there has never been peace. Moreover, this conflict has taken every possible form of violence: land disputes; attacks on farms by individuals; skirmishes between armed guards; rock and knife fights; wars between gangs; wars waged by regular and irregular forces; wars of attrition, terrorism, and anti-terrorism; and full-fledged wars on a broad scale with the most modern weapons known to military history.

Historians can no doubt cite many examples of similarly protracted conflicts. Nations such as the Swiss and the Dutch, which have fought long and hard for their independence, can certainly tell us something about extremely protracted wars of independence. And there are those conflicts which have been dragging on for a very long

time, like the Irish conflict. Although we Jews are very
fond of regarding our fate as unique, there is much to be
gained by viewing our history in the broader context of
world history. Still, that is not a source of much consola-
tion. In recent years the Middle East has become a vast
storehouse of deadly weapons on a scale equal even to that
of the NATO alliance. Should another war break out in the
region it will be terribly destructive, if only because of the
nature of the weapons that will be employed within a relatively limited area.

Nor let it be forgotten that this almost hundred-year
conflict continues and parallels the long-standing historical
conflict between the Jews and the world. The very same elements which characterized that conflict—pushing the Jew
to the margins of history, stripping him of his legitimacy,
the almost all-consuming hatred—are also coming to char-
acterize the conflict in which the State of Israel finds itself.
The same long-standing conflict which had been dispersed
across many countries and which also took all possible
forms—religious, racial, economic, ideological—has, it
seems, focused in recent years in one place, has clothed itself in a distinct and specific political garb, but still drags
into its wake both the wider world and the Jews all over
the world. Few regional conflicts anywhere arouse such
broad international interest.

I sometimes ask myself whether the obduracy of this
conflict perhaps derives from the deep roots of that ancient
struggle between the Jews and the world. And can it be that
secretly we Jews fear the termination of this conflict? For
then we will finally find ourselves at the beginning of a harmonious, or at least essentially normal, relationship with
the world. Do the Jews really want simply to be happy?
wondered Hermann Cohen, the German-Jewish philosopher, when an attempt was made to get him interested in

Zionism. By this question, no less and perhaps even more
than by all his philosophy, he expressed a distinctly Jewish
sensibility. For the Jew fears that something essential to his
identity will be lost if he stands in a normal relationship
with the world. I am not talking here about a spiritual-intellectual debate between the Jew and the world, for I do not
see the Jews as merely spokesmen for one or another spiritual stand. The specific Jewish religion is not the source of
this conflict. And anyway, beliefs and ideas were always a
very relative matter in Jewish life. There were always
different interpretations and explanations, sometimes altogether at odds, of what is called Jewish thought, values,
and positions. But the world did not take an interest in
them, nor did it go to war against them. The heart of the
conflict between the Jews and the world relates primarily
to the existential situation of the Jews, whatever their
views. The nature of Jewish existence in the non-Jewish
world is what has fed the conflict. And since every conflict
involves interaction between two sides, we must ask ourselves about our contribution to this conflict and to what
extent we can reduce it and the damage it does. I never
imagined that the Jews could be regarded as a passive object tossing helplessly on the waves of history. We had and
have views, intentions, deeds. The question is how these
fuel the conflict. It is much more difficult to examine
honestly our contribution to this conflict than to blame
others automatically. It has become our habit to point an
accusing finger at the world and to speak of ourselves in
terms of some undefined Jewish fate that is, unfortunately,
our lot. But that is not the reality. All our efforts, in my
view, must be directed at diminishing the dimensions of the
conflict between us and the world, a conflict that has more
than once brought us to the threshold of almost total destruction. We must realize that we cannot absolve ourselves

by proposing ways to change the world (which obviously needs to be changed), but must also propose ways to change ourselves. Besides, that is more within the range of the possible than is the attempt to change the world.

But that is not my subject here. What I have said is only a general ideological introduction that sets out my basic position regarding the conflict. My real intention in this essay is descriptive, to try to describe what happens in a society that finds itself in a protracted conflict, to examine the positive and negative consequences of this kind of situation. I will try to do this by examining nine basic concepts: survival and war for survival; time; the landscape; central and local; energy; intimacy and freedom; self-righteousness and self-hatred; enlisted art and perspective; and death.

SURVIVAL AND THE WAR FOR SURVIVAL

When analyzing the deep crisis into which Israeli society was plunged following the Yom Kippur War, the sense of despair, the heavy-heartedness, and the self-blame, it seems that the war itself should not have come as a surprise. After all, given the political situation, this war was expected and in a certain sense everyone knew that one day it would break out. Were Belgium, for example, to be attacked today by the Netherlands, the surprise of the war would undoubtedly create a sense of deep crisis. But Israel in fact all along anticipated that war would erupt, with even greater inevitability than the Six-Day War. Those at the rightist end of the political spectrum continuously asserted that the real intention of the Arabs is to destroy the State of Israel and that they are only waiting for the oppor-

tune moment to strike, while on the Left the argument was
that the Arabs will never accept the status quo created
after the Six-Day War, and that they will try to change it
by military means if diplomatic means fail.

Nor did the war reveal any real military weakness. On the
contrary, precisely because it placed us in so dangerous a
lurch, what it revealed was how militarily powerful we actually are. A man's strength is revealed not when he acts in
anticipated situations, according to ready plan, but when
he is caught off guard in an unanticipated situation.

Neither did the war reveal our deep isolation in the
world. This isolation had already begun several years earlier and was not then a cause of special anxiety. In a certain sense the massive aid and support we received from
the United States during the war was unprecedented in our
history. Israel's isolation during the war was diplomatic but
had little practical effect.

Perhaps the sense of depression was brought on by the
large number of losses we suffered. Every loss is dear to us
and scars us deeply. But we are experienced in death and
war and have gone through periods much more difficult in
terms of the toll taken on us. In the War of Independence
the absolute and relative number of losses was immeasurably higher; nevertheless, at that time the air was not so
laden with depression.

Is the reason for the crisis to be found in the so-called
blunder? The time has come to state clearly what that
"blunder" was. It was not political or moral, nor was it related to certain "irregularities" in the armed forces. There
always were "irregularities" in the army, and they did not
prevent it from achieving impressive victories. Nor was the
blunder the result of an error in judgment about when the
war was to break out, because of which the reserves were
not mobilized two or three days earlier.

The blunder was that the security of the State of Israel was based on a system in which an error in human judgment was able to have such fatal consequences.

The Israel Defense Forces' system for absorbing an enemy attack was fundamentally sound in terms of training, arms, level of command, and so on. The problem was that they did not have enough warning time to counter a surprise attack. The IDF should have been organized in such a way that the forces deployed along the borders could by themselves hold off the attackers until the reserves were mobilized, or could disengage from the enemy in such a way that, to overcome this disengagement, the enemy would require the amount of time needed to mobilize the reserves. The blunder lay in a certain military conception, which also has psychological and political roots, and all those responsible for it must be made to pay for their deeds. But that is no reason for a heavy feeling of shock or of a crisis in values.

In my view the main reason for this deep sense of crisis must be sought in the shock of sudden passage from a situation of imagined but pseudo-normality to a situation of total war, that shock which occurred physically between 1:30 and 2:00 P.M. on that historic Yom Kippur afternoon.

Israeli society has constantly asked itself the basic question: What should be the distance and relation between survival and the war for survival? In other words, how much and what of life should be mortgaged to the war for survival and what should be freed for survival itself? A society in a protracted conflict gets accustomed to seeing everything in terms of the requirements of war. Since the threat is total there is a tendency to put all of existence at the service of the war for survival. However, once everything begins to be put in lien for the war, survival itself becomes not worth fighting for; it gets distorted and begins to seem pointless. The major question is that of proportion, of distance, of the distribution of resources, of the extent of spiritual subjugation to the war. A classic example of the dilemma is the banal problem faced by every local council, whether to devote funds for construction of another shelter or to use those funds to build a theater or art gallery.

The Spartan logic is familiar. It is best that we give up something or postpone satisfactions in order to guarantee survival. This logic always finds powerful and persuasive spokesmen in society, against whom stand those who are concerned about the quality of survival, its level, values, and riches, in order not to be totally subjugated to the war.

The pioneering society knew where to draw the line. Material satisfactions were postponed, but spiritual and even material substitutes were developed that were able to help raise the level of existence without impairing the preparations for the war for survival.

The struggle between these two poles leads to repression of the war, and this repression, too, has its own powerful dynamics. The need to create a quasi-normality is clear. In the years preceding the Yom Kippur War, Israel to a certain extent lived a schizoid existence and even made of it a complete world view. During the War of Attrition, when no one could yet envisage its end, an attempt was made to set up a system of normal life alongside the war. The soldiers fighting at the front would say, "We are fighting here so that life in Tel Aviv can go on as if nothing were happening here. When I am discharged I want to join that normal life, and to a certain extent the fact that it exists gives me the strength to be here."

Visitors to Israel during that war were astonished to see the normal life that was being lived here. We are not the first to do this. Many societies have maintained a dual sys-

tem of life in wartime. One need only recall Madrid cele-
brating in its taverns during the Spanish Civil War.

The price paid for this dual existence, which definitely
has certain advantages, is the psychological shock of the
Yom Kippur War. And the psychological shock leads to
military shock. Where precisely to draw the line between
survival and the war for survival is a question Israeli society is still struggling with, for this line is never fixed;
changing circumstances are constantly moving it. But a
fundamental ideological position can at least serve to guide
its placement in changing circumstances. Surprisingly, the
classic distinction between Right and Left does not block
out different positions on this issue. The interests of the
Left and the Right are such that, despite their differences
about the nature of survival and the nature of the war,
both demand that the distance between survival and the
war for survival be narrowed. All shadings of the center, in
the meantime, will try to widen the distance as much as
possible.

TIME

And I had no time
Now it is clear
I had no time

And I had no time
Now it is clear
I had no time

Half my life
Can now be
Silenced
My shadow lengthens
With the sun's march
I'm the man
Who had no time

And I had no time
To grow a tree
Of thoughts
At my pace, slowly
Something more
Understood
Less a potpourri
Of shouts
Of meals taken standing

My life went by from newspaper to newspaper
My breath was winded
In short-distance runs
For His sake

And I had no time
To cover myself with hyssop
Or a shirt
No time for
Birth—burial—birth
To join with memories
Or for the pages of the heavy tome
To yellow

To be understood
Certain
Lost
Gain an inheritance
Between my father and me—the sea

The muster was full
People spoke in first person plural
The days together
At the end of the marches.
A stony moon on the field
Someone nearby turns and black,
Passes the palm of his hand
Across my warm breast
My hand supports the chin
Of some sleeper
And slowly blanches
The weight of a mighty skull
Hair and dreams
My distant wife
My salt wife alone aroused vigilant
And with child.

In this poem Haim Gouri expresses a truly felt sense of time. Time in a society in conflict is not natural time. The conflict distorts the normal sense of time. There is a feeling of tremendous waste of time on things that are neither genuine nor natural. Instead of true inner time there is the time of "newspapers," with its leaps and starts and gaps. The entire process of organic growth is set awry in time of war.

It is the wars, too, that divide time into artificial but highly resistant divisions. Our literary, economic, and social history is divided into periods by the wars. They are bold red lines that mark the end of one period or generation and the beginning of a new. We speak of the War of Independence generation of writers, of the Israeli economy between the Sinai Campaign and the Six-Day War, of the Israeli theater between the last two wars, and so on. The wars become the means par excellence for sorting and demarcating time. But are they the proper yardstick for sorting and measuring complex historical developments? Are they not an external, almost technical, yardstick? A society in conflict, it turns out, does not think so. It measures all around the wars.

The meaning of time is distorted in other ways as well. Personal timetables are also overturned. Like all modern men, the Israeli, too, lives under pressure of time, with the feeling that there is not enough time and that he has to put up a tough struggle to master it. But unlike his Western fellow, the Israeli is thrust into strange periods of dead time in which the normal course of time and his relation to it must undergo change. We saw this clearly after the Yom Kippur War. People manning the front lines for many long months left the normal time cycle. Ordinarily living a crowded, heavy schedule, they suddenly found themselves being submerged in formless, undefined time. They suddenly had to contend with too much time on their hands, had time to think things over, to develop human relationships the likes of which they could not have developed in other situations, time for games and for reading. People found themselves alone on long night watches, far from their families. The balance of the entire normal economy of time was upset. But not only personal time undergoes sharp vagaries in a society embroiled in a conflict. The general, and I would even say metaphysical, conception of time is also most significant in such a society.

From the inception of Zionism, or at least since the Balfour Declaration, we had, it seems, a linear sense of time. We saw time moving forward, bringing us nearer to the solution, and we regarded the passage of time in what was basically an optimistic manner. Time was on our side. The conflict has an end and time brings us, slowly or rapidly, toward its solution. There were perhaps different estimates about where the end is located, about the rate of advance toward it, but basically everyone felt that history was working to our advantage, that in the end we would arrive at the longed-for destination—peace—and that the movement in this direction was ineluctable. As a character in a play by Hanoch Levine put it: "If I didn't know that we were making history, I would never have been able to endure." We all saw ourselves as makers of history, and history has a goal.

After the Yom Kippur War the first signs began to appear of a change in attitude toward the larger course of time: no longer essentially optimistic linear time advancing even if at a wearying pace, but a sense of moving about in an endless circle. An endless rhythm of war-respite-war-respite. Historical movement without goal. The despair of turning in a circle and getting nowhere. An ideology was even developed to interpret this feeling of time: no longer real history with a goal at its end, but a vision of redemption, the end of days, a breaking out of real history. This conception of time also has deep roots in Jewish tradition.

It seems to me that both these conceptions of time in relation to the conflict are incorrect, that after a hundred years of conflict it is apparent that neither of them accurately reflects reality. The correct conception of time must be spiral. Time does not advance straightforwardly toward the solution, nor does it move pointlessly in a circle. There are years and periods when we are nearer to the solution and periods when it is more remote. We move toward and away from the solution, and the point of contact we long for, that tangent of time and the solution, also depends on us.

THE LANDSCAPE

The protracted conflict in Israel has given rise to a sense of being stifled. It is that which impels Israelis to do all they can to travel abroad. People lay out great sums of money, way beyond their means, just to feel what it is like to cross a border and to visit other countries. Travel abroad is a form of status, a kind of privilege. And when the Israeli arrives in some other country he becomes a highly dynamic tourist, constantly on the move, wanting to see as much as possible. There are Israelis who have hardly traveled in their own country but who are super-tourists in the great wide world.

Besides this Israeli claustrophobia, the war has also produced an intimate and profound relationship with the landscape of a kind unknown to the Jew in the *Golah*. Because of the wars, because of the long stints at the lines, because of training and maneuvers, the Israelis have developed a deep and detailed relationship with the immediate landscape around them. I recall a great literary work, perhaps the most important produced in Israel in the last thirty years: S. Yizhar's *The Days of Ziklag*. This work is suffused with a sense of landscape rare even in world literature. A group of soldiers engaged in seven days of fighting on one hill in the northern Negev sinks into an almost mystical experience of landscape, from that close at hand—a ditch, a fold in the ground, a small hut, a wadi—to the broader landscape—the sky, the sunsets, the distant panorama. The landscape experience in *The Days of Ziklag* becomes a substitute for a religious experience.

Not only the fighters themselves (and who here has not

participated in one way or another in the wars?) develop this attitude toward the landscape. One can sometimes see bereaved parents develop a profound and intimate relationship with the site where their son fell, which they often visit. That random hill, ordinary wadi, nondescript dune assumes deep meaning for them. The last place seen by their son is bound up in pain and deep emotion. The rocks, the bushes, the view from there become important, are lifted out of their randomness.

War has deepened the sense of landscape, has brought its details to the fore, and has personalized it. The concept "a place where our blood ran" intermeshes landscape with political ideas. Love and fear, a desire to flee and a desire to establish contact, are powerfully fused in the Israeli's relationship to landscape.

CENTRAL AND LOCAL

War causes tremendous centralization in a society. If the unity of a society is a value—and I am not convinced that it is anything like an absolute value—there is nothing like war to accelerate a society's unity, to mix social classes, to create encounters impossible in times of peace. War gives rise to a vigorous social mobility. As a consequence of his military service every young person in Israel travels the length and breadth of the country and meets people from other parts and other classes. Every annual turn of reserve duty brings diverse social classes together. The war also subjugates all elements of life to one center. Economy, settlement, culture—everything can be tied to it, and the final test of every element is the assistance it can offer to the supreme goal of survival. In the early days of Zionism this link assumed an almost preposterous character, but was extremely serious for the people involved. The newborn goat, the furrow plowed were not matters of slight importance, but a significant addition in the struggle to establish the state. Every detail was woven into the vital fabric of the number one question: Does it assist or work against the war for survival?

However, this strict subjugation to a single center drained the local of its vitality. In a small country where under any circumstances the local has to put up a struggle to survive, such a sense of center further undermined the ability to develop a feeling for the local. The geographical aspect of this exemplifies some of the implications of this phenomenon, but it does not fully encompass it. In a small country like Israel—and I am speaking about Israel in its 1967 borders—entire regions, such as the Negev and the Galilee, are still remote and neglected. There is a constant stream toward the center, even though by European or American standards the distance from the Negev and the Galilee to that center is negligible.

In the world at large, in recent years, processes are at work aimed at strengthening the local sense and at rehabilitating the vitality of regional centers. Faced by the leveling processes of centralization, the result of the constantly improving technological means available to the state machine, and confronted with the unifying power of the media and the lackluster anonymity of the developing world culture, many feel a need to cultivate a local, at least sociocultural, consciousness of region, town, or village. The struggle is for a specific identity and is being accompanied by local, almost tribal awakenings. This struggle is taking place primarily in the domain of culture: the cultivation of local dialects, dress, life-styles, and the like.

ENERGY

A society that lives with a protracted conflict grows accustomed to the fact that war is a source of energy for many things, that it rouses energies from hidden sources in the individual and in society. There is more than a grain of truth in the classic fascist notion that sees in war and strife sources of important energy for human activity in many fields. Stressful and emergency situations create sources of energy unknown and impossible in peaceful circumstances. A person does not have a fixed quantity of energy which, if expended in one realm, is no longer available for another. The conflict, the stress and pressure, awaken imagination and stir creative powers. Had De Gaulle not placed an embargo on Israel and continued instead to supply us with war planes, it is doubtful that we would have found the energy to set up our own outstanding aviation industry, which has successfully developed and is now manufacturing an Israeli fighter plane. The conflict forced us to enter many areas that under conditions of peace we would never have dared enter. In his poem Haim Gouri writes of spiritual energies squandered because of the conflict, but it could be demonstrated that a condition of peace would not release those same energies for other purposes; instead it would have induced in us a passive slumber, and powerful and imaginative energy would simply have been lost.

I recall conversations with soldiers who claimed that it was our good fortune that the Arabs rejected the partition plan in 1947 and forced the War of Independence on us. Because of this war we made territorial, technological, and other gains. Try to imagine the history of the State of Israel during these last thirty years without the conflict. The picture to emerge would likely show a country with much fewer achievements than those made by the Israel which has had to maintain itself in the course of conflict.

I remember a letter written by a young officer who fell at the Suez Canal during the War of Attrition. It was the time of the great student revolts in the West, and the newspapers were filled with reports on the new "youth culture" in the West. This young officer wrote to a friend and tried to compare himself with those other young people. This is more or less what he wrote: "Here I am at the Canal, living with the danger of death, responsible for an artillery battery, responsible for a group of men, in situations of incredible pressure. I have to draw upon all my best physical and spiritual resources. And at the same time what is a young Swiss fellow my age doing? Taking drugs, traveling around, strumming a guitar, demonstrating on environmental issues. I really don't envy him."

This young officer's sensibility was quite common in time of war in Israel, not only as a natural defense mechanism that tries to make a virtue of necessity, but as a complete world view that tries to see the positive side of war, its ability to keep us from too great a preoccupation with the trivial, from immersion in realms that seem nonessential to existence.

This conception, especially when it is accompanied by successes, also created in Israel a fear of peace. And since no one in his right mind would dare to say that he doesn't want peace, language began to be elegantly deceitful. People began to talk about genuine peace, absolute peace, everlasting peace, but not about plain unadorned peace. The concept of peace was shifted to a distant, unattainable, metaphysical plane. In the same way as the Jew in the *Golah* shifted the idea of the return to Eretz Israel to the

days of the Messiah, to the ultimate Redemption, in order
to postpone the actual return to Eretz Israel, so, too, the
spiritual system in Israel began to make of peace something so sublime as to become unattainable.

This conception began to show signs of giving way only
after the Yom Kippur War. It suddenly became apparent
to all that, however good a stimulus war might be for certain kinds of endeavors, it is at the same time destructive of
much that is important. It causes too many things to be
forgotten and neglected. This war bared the ugly and harsh
countenance of the reality of the conflict, even though militarily it was an impressive victory.

A new feeling surfaced that until then had been unknown to Israelis: a feeling of fatigue. Israeli society after
the Yom Kippur War displays the signs of a weighty fatigue.

INTIMACY AND FREEDOM

The protracted conflict has created a society in Israel that
is both intimate and solidary. These are the two most assured values produced as a by-product of the conflict,
values that it seems are very much in demand in the modern world. Intimacy and solidarity are values with which
Jewish history has been quite familiar, but in Israel they
have gained even greater standing. Few societies embroiled
in long-lasting conflicts have attained the level of solidarity
and intimacy achieved by Israeli society. The struggle of
the few against the many has forced the Israelis to develop
an unconditional mutual solidarity, with each the other's
guarantor and each dependent on the other. The narrow
distance between the leadership and the people has also

produced a feeling of intimacy and of participation in basic decisions. The Israelis have, however, had to pay a price for these values. This intimacy has undercut individual liberty; unnecessary concessions have been made in the name of an exaggerated solidarity and a pseudo-intimacy. Moreover, there have always been effective pressure groups that exploit the catchword of solidarity in order to impose a consensus on matters that have nothing to do with the conflict. Although Israel has made impressive achievements in the realms of democracy and individual liberty, the struggle to deepen these was sometimes restricted in the name of a genuine or pseudo-solidarity.

The demand for greater freedom is perceived as a slide toward anarchy endangering the ability to stand up to the difficulties related to the conflict. In recent years Israeli society has been undergoing a process in which individual liberties are being shored up. The vociferous fights for freedom of the press, women's rights, and ecological issues and against police brutality all indicate a growing awareness of individual freedom and rights as an essential counterweight to the power of the regime. Modern history has proved that in a protracted conflict a free society is immeasurably stronger than a totalitarian society. The struggle for freedom is not always pleasant and often seems to erode the sense of solidarity. But freedom and solidarity are not necessarily antinomies.

SELF-RIGHTEOUSNESS AND SELF-HATRED

A society in a protracted conflict, under attack, ceaselessly denounced and defamed, must develop as a mechanism of spiritual defense not only a profound awareness of its justness but also a response to the hostility that surrounds it. Working at high gear, this defense mechanism produces a sense of haughty self-righteousness, a feeling that we are right and the world is mistaken. Seeing yourself as an eternal victim, you begin to believe that being an innocent victim itself makes you somehow more moral. There is a constant need to prove not only that you are not blameworthy but also that the accuser is in fact the guilty one—and not only because of his unjust accusations, but inherently and because of his actions. This feeling has very strong roots in Jewish tradition and of late has become more pronounced in Israel as well.

At the same time, and I think as a necessary corollary of that haughtiness and self-righteousness, an opposite feeling also develops: self-hatred, an attempt to identify with the enemy, to elude him by adopting his positions. This feeling, too, has deep roots in our history. The Jew accuses and hates himself, and since he does not find the strength to leave the Jewish people, he develops self-hatred for the "trap" in which he is caught. It is inconceivable that the whole world is wrong and only we are right. What emerges, then, is total criticism of everything done in Israel; everything appears to be faulty and futile.

These two opposing conceptions complement one another and at the same time link up to one and the same thing: a constantly diminishing sense of reality.

ENLISTED ART AND PERSPECTIVE

The classic saw "When the cannons thunder the muses are silent" is altogether wrong. The life of the arts in Israel proves that a protracted conflict is a powerful stimulus to artistic creation. The production of works of art in Israel is out of all proportion to the size of the population. After the Six-Day War, for example, the newspaper literary supplements were filled with stories and poems written by people for whom this was perhaps the first and last time they produced a literary work. The powerful experiences of the war demanded immediate literary or artistic expression.

By way of generalization it can be said that about half of the artistic creation in Israel in all fields has dealt in one way or another with the "Israeli situation," in which the conflict is central. Novels, stories, poems, plays, films, paintings, symphonic music, cantatas, and other forms of expression deal with issues related to the conflict and include serious attempts to describe the enemy and to plumb his soul.

War is a dramatic and powerful subject that awakens an artistic response. It serves as a meeting ground for secondary themes, is rich in situations of encounter, and is filled with natural tension.

Despite its intensive preoccupation with the subject of war, however, art in Israel has never been a conscripted art, and in that sense has escaped one of the snares set along its path. The call to enlist literature and art is quite common in societies that find themselves in a state of war. Literature and art in Israel have nevertheless on the whole known how to reject even the legitimacy of such a call. It can perhaps be said that because the artists in Israel have been enlisted as citizen-soldiers, they could be free in their creations. Because they were awarded no privileges, were not released from their civic obligations, they purchased in full their artistic liberty.

Writers and poets who during the Yom Kippur War or immediately thereafter announced that they did not want to write a word about the war, that they wanted to ignore it altogether, found their decision accorded not only artistic and social but also profound moral legitimation.

Although the demand to enlist literature was resoundingly rejected, literature and art could not absolve themselves from having to deal with the conflict for reasons of "lack of perspective." When art did take up the subject of the war, out of a sense of personal freedom, it had to do so without accepted artistic perspective. The surrender of perspective is the price art and literature must pay for their own inner response to deal immediately with events. Whoever postpones dealing with current events, because of his search for perspective, loses out on both accounts: the rapid flow of events undermines the tranquillity afforded by perspective even when it is finally found. Thus, when someone waited too long to write about the Six-Day War, hoping to be able to understand it better from a distance attained in time, the Yom Kippur War came and whisked away the subject. The vitality of the experience of the Six-Day War was blotted out by an even more powerful experience, and its significance now assumed different dimensions. Whoever, before writing about the Yom Kippur War, waited to achieve a suitable perspective of time and place—before he found that perspective, Sadat had visited Israel, the peace process had begun, and the impact of a different, new, opposite experience caused the experience of the war to fade.

This, of course, does not mean that one day a literature dealing with recent and more remote past events will not be written from some new genuine perspective. But the vertiginous dynamism of Israeli reality and the chain of dramatic turnabouts have made of the search for perspective an obstacle for that literature which did seek to respond to the "Israeli situation."

DEATH

War ultimately is also a confrontation with death. The greatest and most dreadful danger facing a society in a protracted conflict is that it may become accustomed to the reality of death.

The strength of Israeli society has been that as long as this conflict has been going on, it has generally refused to accept death. Every death was met with shock, anger, and nonacceptance. Although the national ideological system could justify and explain each death as necessary, as the inevitable price of the struggle for survival, there was always tension between the justification of death and sacrifice in the overall context of a society fighting for its life, and the horrendous injustice of the death of a specific individual. The tension and distance between these were always underscored.

There were many ways by which the blow of death could have been softened. Someone once made the calculation that the number of persons killed in all of Israel's wars from its founding to the present is about half the daily number herded into the gas chambers of Auschwitz. But attempts of this kind to console are usually rejected. Precisely because behind the State of Israel is a history in which so much Jewish blood was spilt, and this generation has seen a third of the nation destroyed, every additional death adds to a cup already overflowing, and the pain has been intensified.

Israeli society has wondered whether or not it should prepare its people for death. Societies in an extended conflict such as ours have tried to prepare their people for

the possibility of their death, enlisting for that purpose
magnificent-sounding and sophisticated arguments. I may
be mistaken, but it seems to me that here no attempt was
ever made to tell soldiers that they must be prepared to die,
that some of them will have to sacrifice their lives. We
never had suicide units, although candidates for such units
can also be found in Israeli society. The kamikaze notion is
totally alien to Israeli society. The most dangerous and
complicated missions deep in enemy territory were always
planned together with rescue and retreat contingencies. As
a rule the number of losses in such missions was extremely
low, for in them the rescue system was most highly sophisticated and developed (e.g., the Entebbe operation).

Sadat's remark before the Yom Kippur War that he was
prepared to sacrifice a million Egyptians to liberate his territory was utterly foreign to us. No one, not even the most
ardent adherents of a Greater Israel, would dare say that
the lives of Israelis must be sacrificed in order to maintain
the unity of Jerusalem, for example. That kind of talk is
impossible among us. People talk, not in terms of self-
sacrifice, but only in terms of defending their lives. Death,
of course, does come, but no one prepares himself for it.
The fine line between repression of death and its nonacceptance is, as a rule, maintained. We have not repressed
death, but neither have we come to accept it.

Often attempts have been made to apply to the Israeli
situation the greatest and most important Jewish myth: the
Akedah, the binding of Isaac. Despite the many attempts
of this sort, and despite the fact that art and literature have
used metaphors borrowed from this myth, I believe that
basically it is irrelevant to the true feeling of Israeli reality.
The fathers have not sent their sons to death in the name of
some idea. First of all, the fathers themselves went to fight a
war, the justice of which they thoroughly clarified to them-

selves, and the sons followed the fathers of their own free will, not on behalf of anybody else. Here the situation was in no way that of an all-knowing, believing father sending his passive son off to slaughter. The myth of the *Akedah* was much more applicable to the acts of martyrdom, of sanctification of the Name, performed in the *Golah* in the Middle Ages. There the model of the myth was applicable; here it is essentially irrelevant.

While there is no preparation for death, when it does come a ritual is created around the dead. I view this ritual as an extremely important antidote to becoming accustomed to the war situation. The ritual of producing memorial books for the fallen has become a matter of utmost importance. The need for some form of verbal perpetuation testifies not only to the traditional Jewish respect for the written word but also to the depth of the memory that is preserved. I recall the touching story of a bereaved father who approached a writer and asked him to prepare a memorial book for his fallen son. The writer asked him for material that might help in the preparation of the book— letters, a personal diary, essays, and the like. The father said, "Regrettably, I don't have such material. My son never kept a diary and his few letters are short and laconic. But he was a superb mathematician. Perhaps we can print some of the mathematical problems he knew how to solve." The story is pathetic but shows to what depths the need to perpetuate memory reaches. It is also customary in Israel to publish pictures of the fallen soldiers in the daily newspapers, along with brief biographical sketches. I don't know if there are many societies that have acted similarly in protracted war situations. I remember how the American media reported the deaths in Vietnam, the weekly toll squeezed in between reports of traffic accidents and sports items. It is not surprising that that war ended for the

United States as it did. In most countries a laconic tele-
gram serves to inform families that one of theirs has fallen.
Here families were informed by a committee of people spe-
cially trained for it.

The War of Attrition confronted Israel with a severe
problem in contending with death. In a certain sense, that
problem continues to vex as a result of daily terror, although not to the same extent. Paradoxically, it has been
easier for Israeli society to contend with a large number of
deaths resulting from a short war that also had clear
achievements, such as the Sinai Campaign and the Six-Day
War, than to deal daily with a much smaller death toll but
one seemingly without purpose, bringing no gain, without a
sense of an end, just from holding the lines, as was the case
in the War of Attrition. The experience of that war had
very bitter consequences for morale, and Israel's policy
makers vowed that they would not allow Israel to be drawn
into another war of attrition and would immediately try to
escalate it into a full-fledged war.

But even in the course of that war it was possible to see
how Israeli society tried to soften the impact of the constant presence of death. Toward the end of the period the
pictures of the fallen had already been shifted from the
front page of the newspapers to some inside page, the pictures becoming smaller, the text more concise.

It was a complicated process, for the repression of the
presence of death is highly dangerous for a society in a
conflict. It gives rise to an inner toxin that is liable to have
the gravest consequences. For even the briefest texts could
not conceal how heavy a price was being paid and how
great was the pain. I remember a text of that sort which
appeared toward the end of the War of Attrition. It
was terse, but encompassed an awful tragedy. "Lieut.
Moshe K., 22, was brought to burial yesterday in his

kibbutz, Lohamei Ha-Gettaot [the Ghetto Fighters], in a full
military ceremony. He was killed at the Suez Canal on Tues-
day evening, two days before his discharge and several
days before he was to be married. Earlier in his military
service he had been wounded. He leaves a mother, a widow
who lost two of her sons in the Holocaust in Europe."

That's all. But what a cruel tragedy is contained within
these few lines. We must mourn grievously, deeply. Only
thus can we pursue peace with all our strength.

In recent years, in the period following the Yom Kippur
War, words and concepts charged with a religious meaning
have begun to make their way into our language. This is
related to the general neo-Judaic process that has been
sweeping over many areas of our life. Interpretations of a
religious character have been given to the deaths of those
who have fallen. Even the classic text of the official obitu-
ary has been changed in a religious direction. Concepts
such as "By his death he has sanctified the Name" have
begun to appear in the language of the funeral orators, especially military rabbis. The fatigue that has settled over
the national system resulting from the endless toll of death
taken from us is understandable. And the political situation is no longer so clearly a struggle for survival. However, the religious system's entry into the national system is
extremely dangerous. The soldiers were not and will not be
killed to sanctify the Name, because the conflict between
us and the Arabs is not over the existence of this or that
God. Just as it is dangerous that the Arabs declare that
their war is to sanctify the name of Allah, it is dangerous
for us to collaborate with this tendency of theirs and to
convert a national-territorial conflict into a religious-met-
aphysical conflict. The notion of sanctification of the
Name was suited to Jewish situations in the *Golah*, where
the dispute was really about the Christians' attempts to

force us to convert. The collective suicide of the Jews then was in fact to sanctify the Name. It was done in order to remain loyal to their faith. But here we are engaged in a national, not a religious, struggle. Should it be drawn into the religious realm, it may well never come to an end.

This essay was written in 1975, when peace was very remote. But now it is actual. From the moment of Sadat's visit here and his declaration of Egypt's readiness to recognize Israel, I knew that a new historical process from which there is no retreat had begun.

The peace treaty has been signed. But it is only the beginning of a new road. This road, if we want to take it to where it can lead, requires basic change in several fundamental concepts with which we have lived for generations. It requires that we change our image of ourselves. It should not be forgotten that a mechanism suited to a most protracted conflict has been created and has given rise to its own world view. The slow transition from a basically abnormal to a normal situation is painful and problematic. We have displayed many fine qualities of spirit in a situation of conflict. Will we know how to convert them to the qualities of spirit required by a situation of peace? Normal situations are gray and banal and lack the ecstatic peaks of situations of conflict. Will we also know how to bring forth the best that is within us in lackluster situations? Without profound inner spiritual changes we will not be able to meet the challenge of external political changes. I believe that the potential creative forces in Israel in a situation of peace are no less than those which have revealed themselves in the situation of war.

DATE DUE